IMAGES
of America

CRYSTAL LAKE

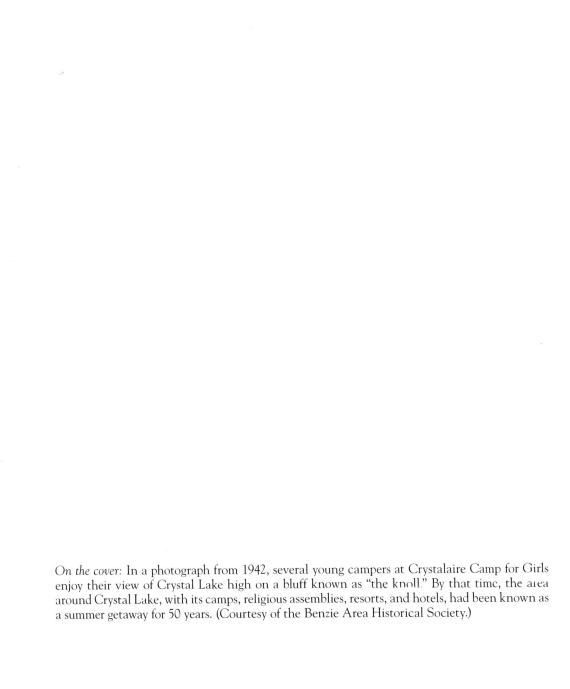

On the cover: In a photograph from 1942, several young campers at Crystalaire Camp for Girls enjoy their view of Crystal Lake high on a bluff known as "the knoll." By that time, the area around Crystal Lake, with its camps, religious assemblies, resorts, and hotels, had been known as a summer getaway for 50 years. (Courtesy of the Benzie Area Historical Society.)

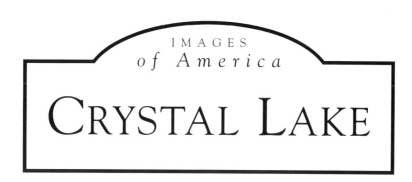

IMAGES
of America
CRYSTAL LAKE

Dr. Louis Yock for the
Benzie Area Historical Society

ARCADIA
PUBLISHING

Copyright © 2009 by Dr. Louis Yock for the Benzie Area Historical Society
ISBN 978-0-7385-6176-9

Published by Arcadia Publishing
Charlesto, South Carolina

Printed in the United States of America

Library of Congress Control Number: 2008926310

For all general information contact Arcadia Publishing at:
Telephone 843-853-2070
Fax 843-853-0044
E-mail sales@arcadiapublishing.com
For customer service and orders:
Toll-Free 1-888-313-2665

Visit us on the Internet at www.arcadiapublishing.com

Contents

Acknowledgments   6

Introduction   7

1.   Benzonia   9

2.   Beulah   33

3.   Cottages, Resorts, and Camps   57

4.   Frankfort and Elberta   95

Acknowledgments

A book such as this is an unintentional result of many eyes, hands, minds, and years of effort. My work of a few short months was made much easier by the people who preceded me at the Benzie Area Historical Museum, specifically the hundreds of volunteers, most of whom I never knew or met, who collected, cataloged, and organized the archival photographs and documents. From my time, I must thank Pete Sandman and Florence Bixby, the two true historians of the Benzie area whose knowledge, try as hard as I may, I will never be able to proximate. Furthermore, I thank Bill Pearson, whose in-depth knowledge of the museum's collection made my digging around much easier and whose further work will only make me regret what I overlooked and failed to include. I need to also thank Jane Purkis, the one I turn to most often to find me the person who knows, to dig through the boxes to get just the right picture, and who otherwise is always there to bridge the gaps in what I think I know.

INTRODUCTION

When the first Yankee settlers arrived at Crystal Lake, the last thing they imagined was that their religious, academic, and industrial enterprises would turn into a vacation paradise for thousands of people. The history of this dramatic pivot is chronicled in the archival pictures and records of the Benzie Area Historical Museum in Benzonia, which is the source for all the photographs in this book. The earliest photographs from the 1860s and 1870s depict Crystal Lake and its towns surrounded by clear-cut forests, lumber mills, and college halls. The glass negatives and panoramic pictures from 30 years on show that along with locomotives and steamships came dance pavilions, casinos, hotels, and cottages. Diaries, letters, and postcards switch from recording board feet measurements of lumber to the number of chicken dinners served at resort hotels.

About nine miles long and two miles wide, Crystal Lake was originally unfit for both industry and recreation. Its sheer drop-offs at the base of large hills, together with the swampy ground that buttressed other drop-offs, prompted the Native Americans to utilize other, more convenient, lakes in the vicinity. Having no major river feeding it, and with no outlet to Lake Michigan, it was a large, landlocked lake, considered unusable when the first European and African American settlers were seeking ways to make a living from the natural resources of northwest Michigan. The closest river, the Betsie, was virtually unnavigable, and as Crystal Lake was well off the major trading routes, trails and roads were decades away from approaching it. When viewed from high on a hill, the lake's rich blue beauty set among the green pines and scarlet maples was unsurpassed; however, the people of the mid-19th century were not yet able to make a living selling views.

When the Congregationalists from Oberlin, Ohio, led by the Reverend Charles E. Bailey, chose one of the hills overlooking Crystal Lake for their new town and college in 1858, they were simply happy with the availability of the land and natural loveliness of the lake. About the same time the developers of Frankfort, who settled a little south and west of Crystal Lake on a commercially viable harbor, came with an entrepreneurial spirit to take advantage of the timber and their site's access to Lake Michigan. Neither group saw in Crystal Lake the bounty it would eventually bring their descendants. It was the attempt to cut a channel between Crystal Lake and Lake Michigan in 1873, which resulted in Crystal Lake's lowering, that changed the geography of the lake and the future for those settled around its shores. Without the swampland and drop-offs, and with gently sloping sandy beaches, perspectives on the usefulness of the lake changed. The arrival of the railroad to Crystal Lake in 1887 brought hopes for an increase of growth in Benzonia's Congregational college, an increase for Frankfort's industry, and, new for both communities, city people seeking cool lake breezes during the summer.

The photographs of the Benzie Area Historical Museum chronicle the waves of businesses and industry that came and went over the last century and a half. They show how timber and railroads grew together and caused the region to prosper and how by the time the lumber boom ended, Frankfort had established itself as a major railroad port on Lake Michigan as well as launched industries that would carry it beyond timber. Along Frankfort's shores were seen ovens forging iron ore into steel, depots where fruits from the local orchards were packaged and shipped, and docks where the commercial fisherman tied up their tugs. History was less kind to Benzonia, where snapshots of grand college buildings offered high hope but now appear more like ghostly reminders of what was never meant to be. While the camera recorded the booms and the busts, the newer modes of transportation replacing the older ones, the depressions and recessions, and the rust belt oxidizing, it also recorded the changing styles of the one industry that began with the lowering of Crystal Lake and has been present since—tourism and recreation. The people and their concerns may have come and gone, but the natural beauty of Crystal Lake remained constant. Through the four distinct seasons, Crystal Lake has always offered something to those choosing to spend some time along its shores.

The scope of this book is simply to share the pictures and information acquired by the Benzie Area Historical Museum as they pertain to the towns, villages, and resorts that developed on Crystal Lake from the 1850s through the 1940s. Choosing the pictures for such a book is a difficult task as so many people have been generous in their photographic contributions to the Benzie Area Historical Society since 1969. This book is drawn from an embarrassment of riches. Unfortunately though, editorial decisions had to be made, and so many important and interesting pictures dealing with homes, industry, and families were not included. With the museum's collection, individual photographic books could easily be compiled on Benzonia, Frankfort, and Elberta, as well as homes, families, farms, cottages, and businesses from the area. Since this publication covers many aspects of the area surrounding Crystal Lake, it is perhaps best to view it as an anthology of pictures rather than as a definitive study. It is certainly enough to whet the appetite and make a person seek out that which has not been included. As more pictures are discovered and copies given to the museum's archives, the richness of the photographic history of Crystal Lake and the Benzie area will only grow and be better preserved. Hopefully this book will inspire all who are in some way attached to the Benzie area, as year-round residents, as passers through, or as those who would like to visit, to better appreciate the rich history and unique story of Crystal Lake.

One

BENZONIA

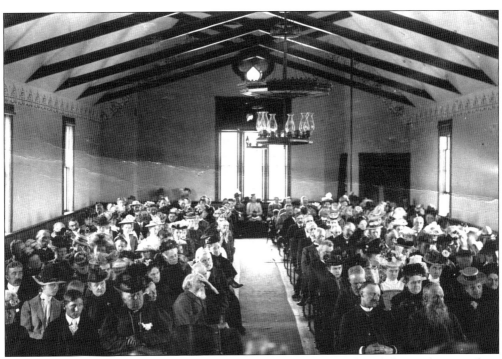

In 1858, on a hill overlooking the lake, the village of Benzonia was founded as a religious colony through the efforts of the Reverend Charles E. Bailey (1822–1894). A Congregational pastor and alumnus of northern Ohio's Oberlin College, Bailey was eager to repeat the success of his alma mater, a renowned college built in largely unsettled country. Bailey convinced family members and friends to join him in the undertaking. The colonists' "Articles of Agreement and Plans for a Christian Colony and Institution of Learning" provided that a quarter of the stockholders' lands were to establish and endow the college. Well into the 20th century, the Congregational church's services, events, and moral attitudes were at the center of Benzonia.

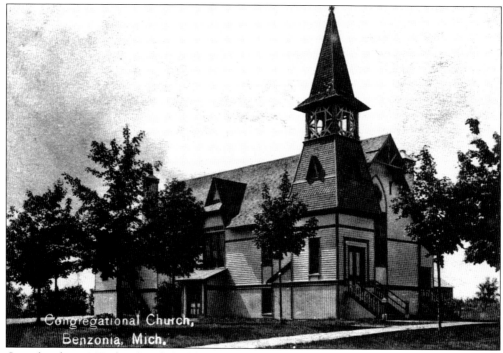

Completed in 1887, the church building (top, as seen from the east) was the focal point of the religiously minded residents. To accommodate the growth in membership an addition was added in 1914 (bottom, as seen from the west). Under the leadership of the Reverend Harlow S. Mills, pastor from 1896 to 1916, the Benzonia Congregational Church became the headquarters of the "greater parish," which served area Congregational churches, schools, and meeting halls on an itinerant basis. The building remained the Congregational church until 1968, when a new building was erected. Dorothy Hensel, as the sole surviving descendant of the pioneer Charles E. Bailey and a founding member of the Benzie Area Historical Society, arranged for the old church and property to be given to the historical society. Since 1969, it has been the Benzie Area Historical Museum.

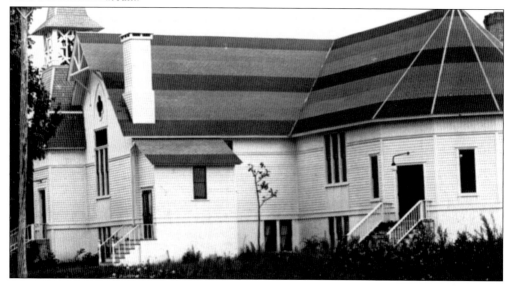

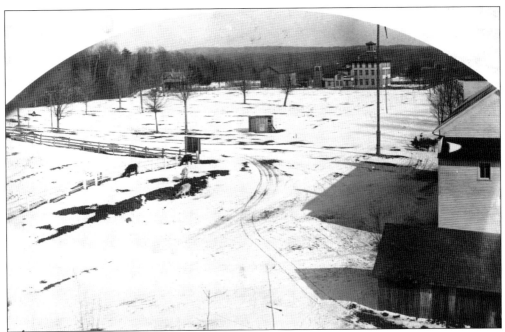

A c. 1889 photograph taken from the church belfry shows the rural nature of the new colony and its moderate success, complete with cows pasturing on the college campus. The flagpole stands in the middle of what is today the intersection of U.S. 31 and Traverse Avenue, and what came to be known as East Hall is seen in the background.

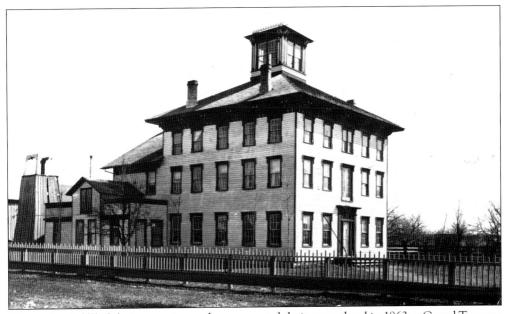

The settlers fulfilled their intention and incorporated their new school in 1863 as Grand Traverse College. When the college's first and only building burned down in 1874, Charles E. Bailey's brother, John, sold his hotel to the college to be used as its residence and classrooms. As the girls' dormitory and classrooms, it came to be known as East Hall and was destroyed by fire in 1909.

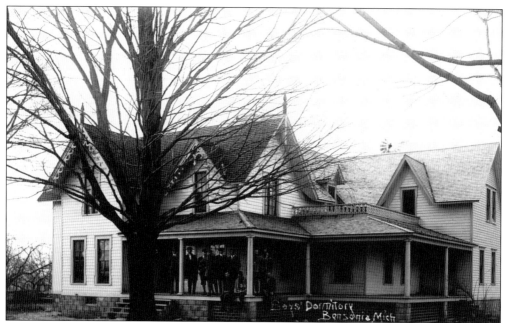

One of the village's earliest buildings was erected in 1859 by Charles E. Bailey. Eventually known as Bailey Cottage, it served simultaneously as a private residence, school, post office, and general store. In the 1890s, the large house was sold and turned into the boys' dormitory for the college. One of its final uses before being torn down in the early 1960s was as the Crossways Tea House.

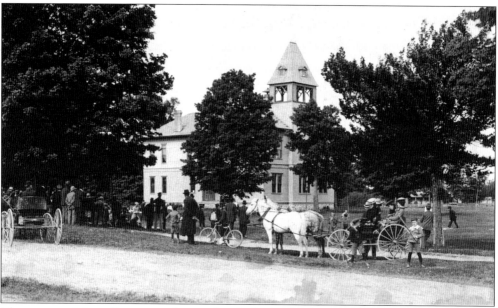

The success of the college seemed assured with the lumber boom, the arrival of the railroad in 1887, and Benzonia's designation as the Congregational Church's regional school. In 1890, Grand Traverse College was renamed Benzonia College. Barber Hall was erected to accommodate the expected increase in enrollment. Standing on Bailey Street until shortly after World War I, it contained a recitation hall, a library room, a laboratory, a museum, and a chapel.

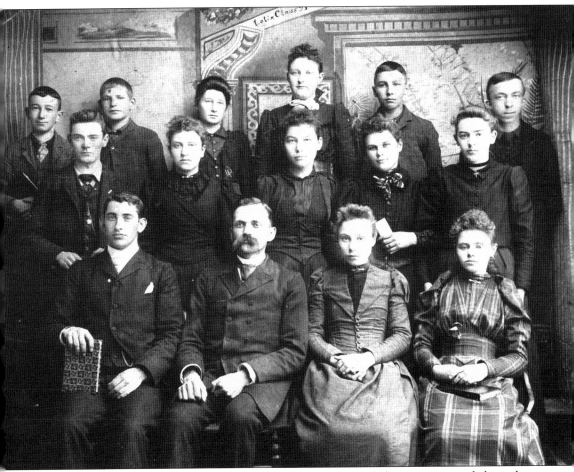

Considered progressive by 1850s standards, the pioneers who settled Benzonia were dedicated to abolition, temperance, and the advancement of universal education. To this end, their college was chartered "to afford to both sexes, without distinction of color, the opportunity of acquiring a liberal education." Pictured above is the 1891 Latin class, or today what would be considered a college preparatory class, of both young men and women.

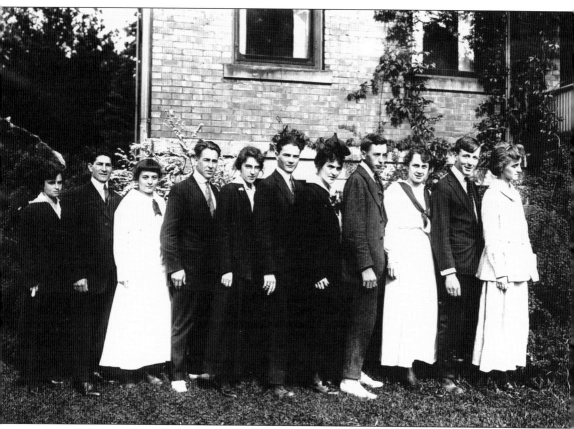

Second from right is Bruce Catton with his 1916 Benzonia Academy graduation class. The academy's most famous alumnus, he went on to be a Pulitzer Prize–winning Civil War author and a 1977 recipient of the Presidential Medal of Freedom. Of the atmosphere and sense of purpose of the little college town, Catton reminisced that growing up in Benzonia was like growing up with the 12 apostles for next-door neighbors.

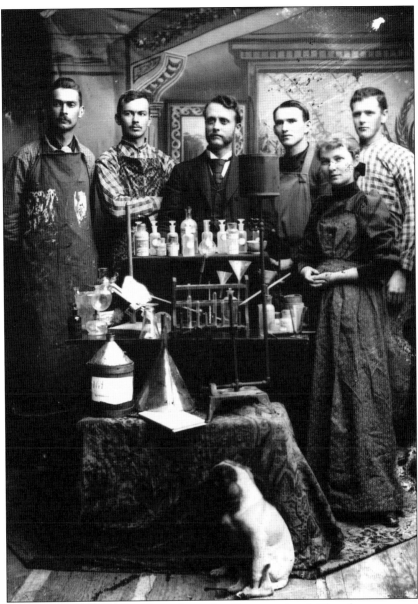

After 1890, the expected support from the wider Congregational Church never materialized; this along with the end of the lumbering boom and Benzonia's isolation from major population centers prevented the college from developing the needed financial base, faculty, and student body. In the fall of 1900, the school underwent its final name change to Benzonia Academy and operated until 1918 as a college preparatory high school. This picture of the Benzonia College chemistry class taken sometime before 1900, with (from left to right) Ward Knight, Willard Waters, Professor Clark, Frank Mott, James Metlard, and Winifred Waters, bears witness to the community's dedication to a high-quality education for its coed students. While the challenges of creating a college in the north woods of Michigan proved to be greater than the good intentions of Benzonia's founders, the value placed on education was successfully instilled and many of the village's sons and daughters, from both the public school and the academy, would go on to receive college educations.

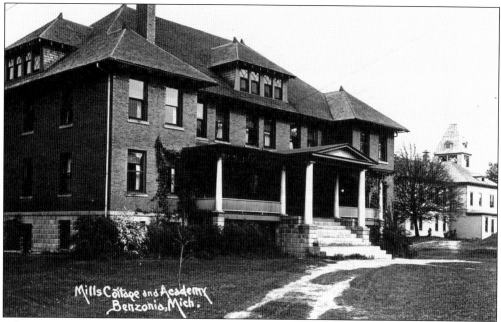

After East Hall burned in 1909, Mills Cottage was constructed as the girls' dormitory and named in honor of Harlow S. Mills, the much-loved and long-tenured pastor of the Benzonia Congregational Church. The building also served for a time as the residence for the headmaster of the academy, George R. Catton, and his family, including his son Bruce. Barber Hall is seen in the background.

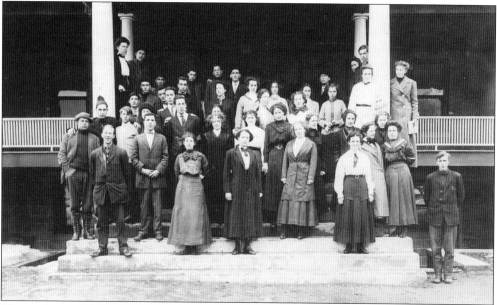

The students of Benzonia Academy pose on the front steps of Mills Cottage in 1910 or 1911. After the academy closed in 1918, the old dormitory was used for several functions, including the high school gymnasium and theater. In 1925, it became the Mills Community House, and it is the only remaining structure of the academy, serving today as the Benzonia Public Library, the community theater, and a meeting hall.

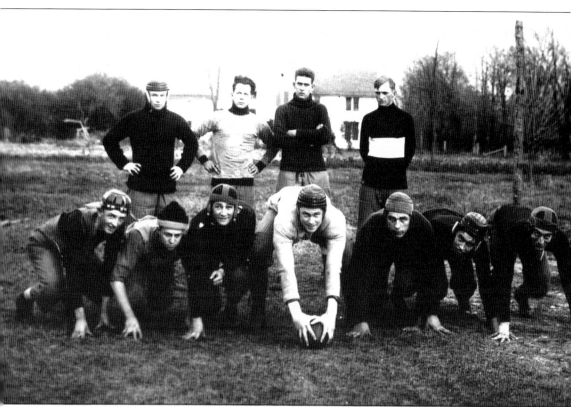

Sports played a major role in the life of Benzonia, and as in all things in the village, religion was never far away. "The Heathen Game" is written, tongue-in-cheek, on a postcard showing the 1913 academy football team. Unfortunately for its sports fans, the enthusiastic teams fielded by Benzonia were never a dominant force in the region's competitions.

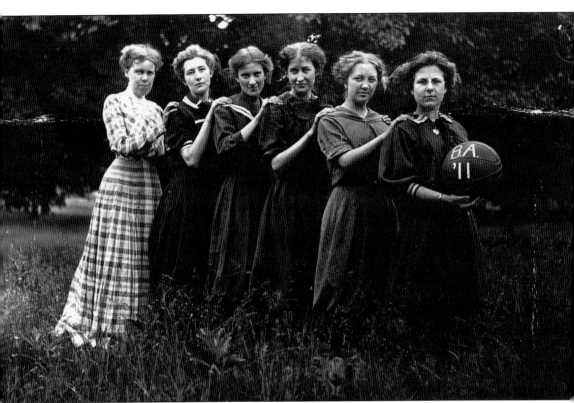

After a long launch ride and an early-morning breakfast on Crystal Lake, the 1911 members of the Benzonia Academy Girls' Basketball team pose for their picture. Dedicated as the residents were to serving the good and humanity, many worked in the mission fields. First on the left is Anna Gertrude Reed, who would eventually serve as a missionary in China.

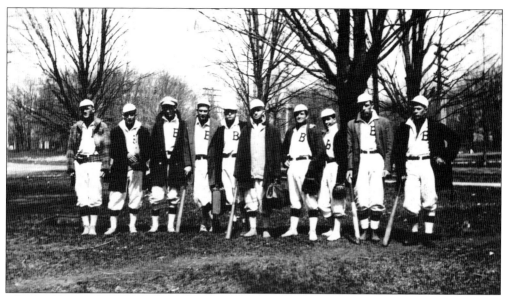

Always able to anticipate a good turnout of spectators, Benzonians particularly liked baseball, a fairly new game to the north woods of Michigan at the dawn of the 20th century. Despite the fact that the ballplayers from Benzonia were noted for not drinking, chewing tobacco, or cursing (too much), divine providence tended to favor their opponents.

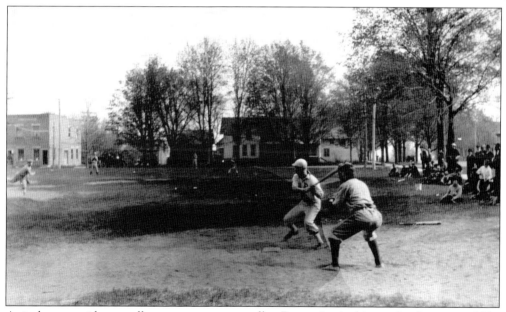

As is the case with any college town, even as small as Benzonia, rivalries and jealousies would be played out on the field. The town with a college became a special mark, and beating it became a source of pride for the visitors. It is reported that the Congregationalist fans (right) did their part by rattling the visiting team with insults. Bailey Cottage, the boys' dormitory, is seen in the background.

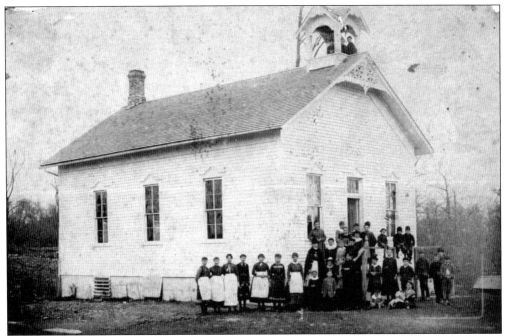

A picture from 1880 shows teacher Maggie Bailey (in front of window) with her students at the Benzonia Township school. Before this structure was erected, various buildings served as the common school where the ungraded students were graduated after they had finished McGuffey's sixth reader. When the population grew and class grades were introduced, a single building became too small and classes were split between this building and East Hall.

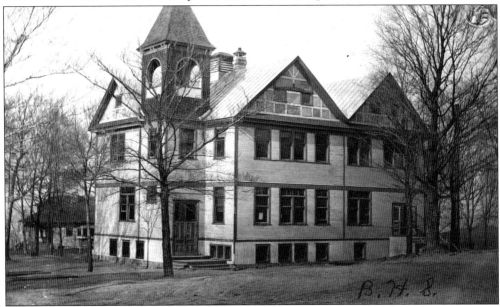

People were dissatisfied with the school divided between East Hall and the small Benzonia School, and so a single building for all the students was erected. Built in 1894, the Benzonia High School served all grades for both Benzonia and Beulah. It graduated its first class of five students in 1898 and would be used until it was torn down after consolidation in the 1960s.

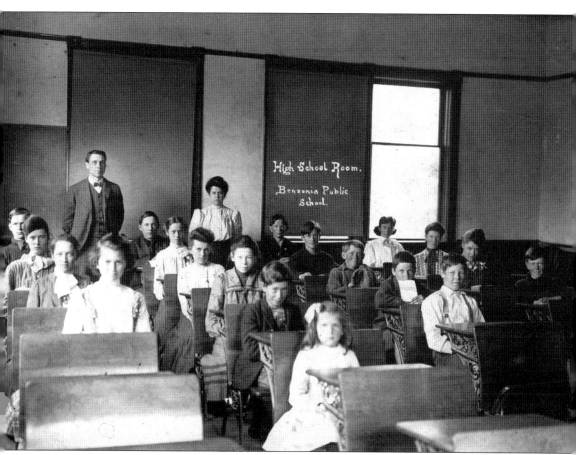

Until 1918, Benzonia had two schools, the academy and the public school (above). This caused some competition and "town and gown" issues. While almost everyone who settled in Benzonia was connected to the Congregational church, not all its residents would necessarily associate themselves with the college or choose to send their children to the academy.

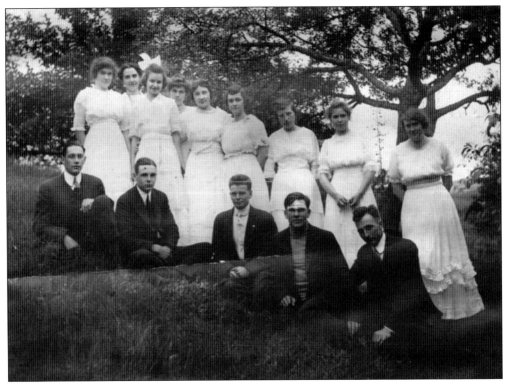

Never graduating more than nine students before 1915, there was a debate about whether or not to eliminate the upper grades at Benzonia High School. The close of the academy in 1918 settled the problem when the public school became the only option. Seen above is the Benzonia High School graduating class of 1915. The white graduation gown was the standard apparel for the graduating young women.

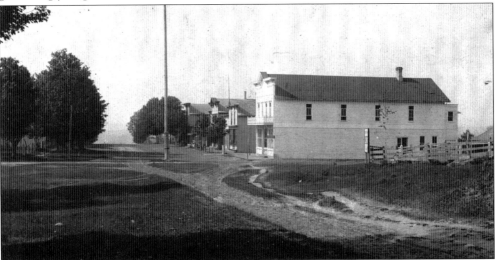

Looking south on what is now U.S. 31, Case's Hall is seen in the foreground with the burgeoning village around 1887. The naming of the village itself is witness to the ideals of its academic-minded founders, the word *Benzonia* being described by its author, Dr. J. B. Walker, as a Latin and Greek hybrid for "a good place to live."

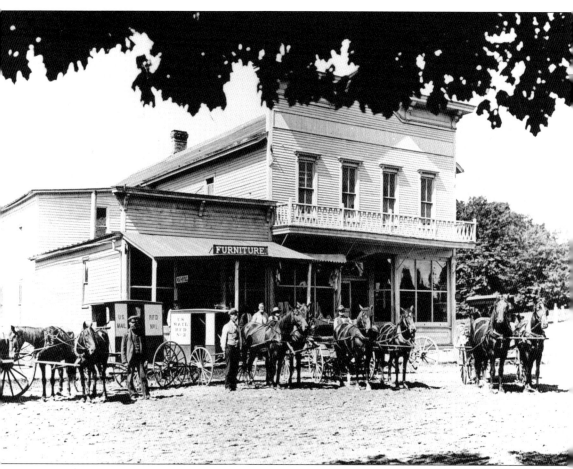

Next to the Congregational church, the steeple of which can be seen in the background, the center of the village's social and political activity often revolved around the Case Mercantile Company. At various times it contained a combination of a general store, furniture store, post office, and upstairs hall for meetings. The mail carriers and their wagons are pictured in front.

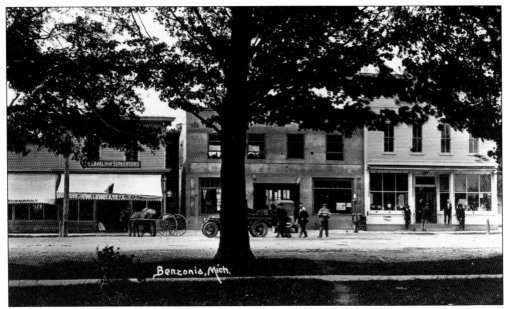

While the stores on Main Street may have been well stocked with goods, one item that would not be found on their shelves was liquor. In the colony's 1858 articles of agreement, it was stipulated that "all conveyances of colony land were to contain a clause forever prohibiting on them the manufacture, sale, or gift, except strictly for mechanical and medicinal purposes, of all intoxicating liquor." This restriction applied to the village well into the 20th century. As the tourist industry grew, the citizens of the village were defeated in their attempts to keep the entire county dry. Expressing his sentiments on the outcome of one of these elections, George R. Catton, the principal of the academy and one staunchly opposed to liquor, mentioned that he felt like Lazarus because he knew what it was like to be "licked by dogs."

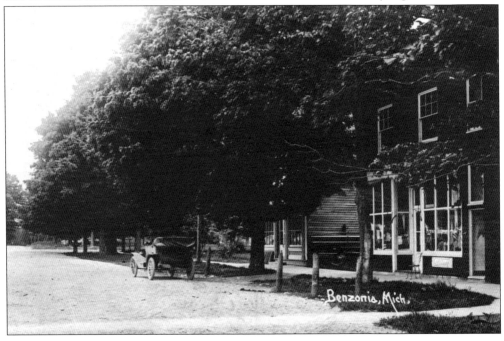

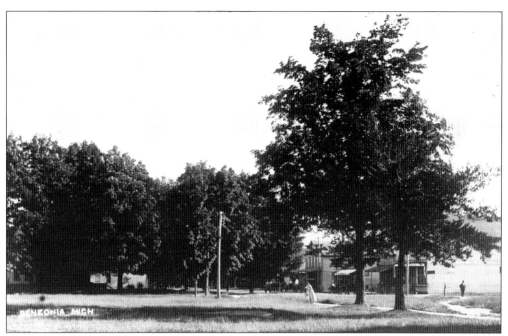

Living high on a hill before modern running water meant either collecting water in a cistern or walking to the town pump. As cistern water was easily and often contaminated, the sweetest water could be found at the town pump (lower right-hand corner). Harold Sprout, son of the local banker, reported that it took 100 strokes to bring the water to the surface and 50 more to fill a three-gallon bucket.

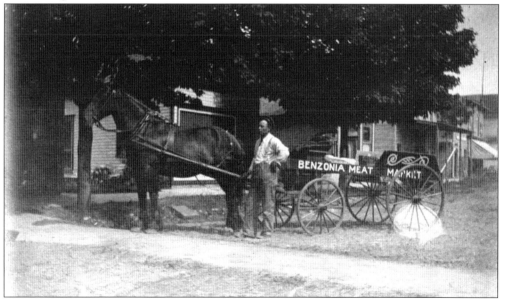

The automobile did not appear in Benzonia until 1908, and according to witnesses its chain transmission made it more of a glorified bicycle. After they became more common, cars could only be used in the summer due to the inability to plow roads. The delivery of all goods by horse and wagon, like the Benzonia Meat Market, was common until the 1920s, when roads and road maintenance began to improve.

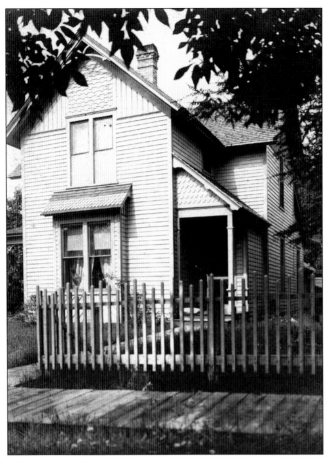

One of the more storied residences in Benzonia is the Sprout House, built around 1888 by the town banker George Sprout. Bruce Catton, in his memoir *Waiting for the Morning Train*, records Sprout carrying deposits between the bank and his home for overnight safekeeping. Sprout's bank building takes center stage in another village legend as the site where a loose black scarf was tied to its door after being found blowing in the street, in the hope that the owner would find it. Mistaken by the Reverend Dunn as a sign of mourning for Mrs. Sprout, he was much shocked and put out when after scurrying to the Sprout home to offer his condolences, he found her answering the front door.

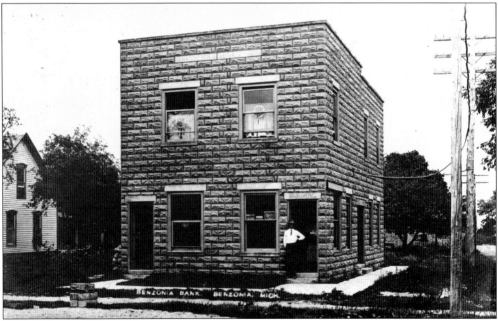

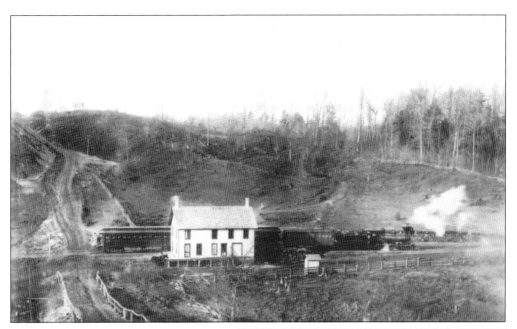

The Benzonia train station sat at the base of East Hill (above). Every direction from Benzonia offered a slope for sleds and toboggans. Due to traffic and trains, the road going north to Beulah was closed to sledders. A fast, steep alternative was East Hill, which was only a slightly less dangerous thrill considering the train tracks at its base. Confident of knowing the railroad schedule, adventurers often chose East Hill for their recreation. Losing control and spilling off the sled, or slamming into a drift to miss a train or sleigh, was a story frequently told by the speed seekers.

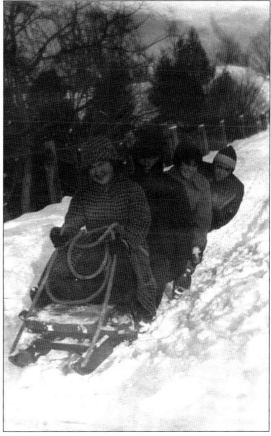

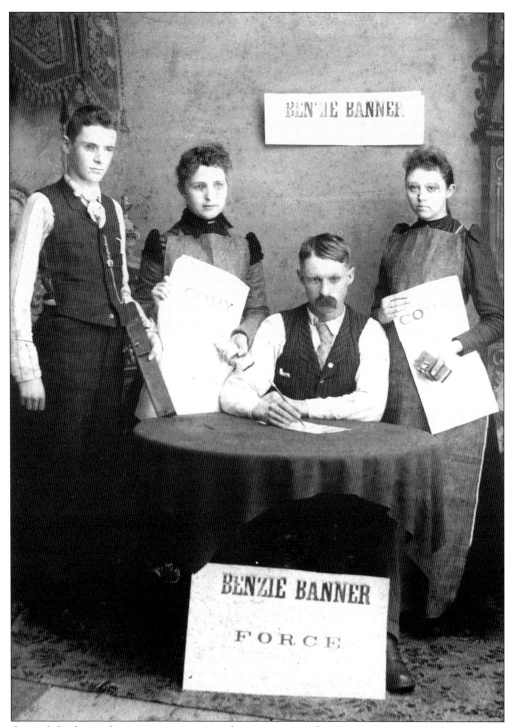

One of the longer-lasting newspapers in the county was the *Benzie Banner*, which contained advertisements and news about the new resorts being built. Pictured from left to right in this 1890 photograph are Eugene C. Case, former owner, publisher, and editor of the newspaper; Ivy Green; E. Gilbert, then publisher; and Nelly Schofield.

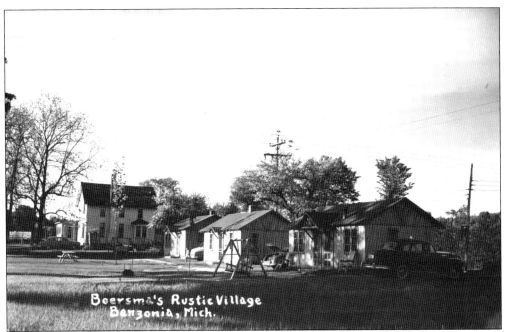
Boersma's Rustic Village, Benzonia, Mich.

Benzonia for most of its history did not try to capitalize on being a resort town, as most of that business went down the hill to Beulah and around the shores of Crystal Lake. With the automobile, camping along the Betsie River and cabins along the highway were established, including Boersma's Rustic Village, later Rosier's Motel. Unlike the lakeshore summer resorts, these motels and cabins were open year-round and were affordable to the factory workers from the industrialized regions of Michigan, Illinois, Ohio, and Indiana. With this new middle-class wealth and mobility came increased tourism and weekend stays for fall hunters, fishermen, and eventually winter snowmobilers and skiers.

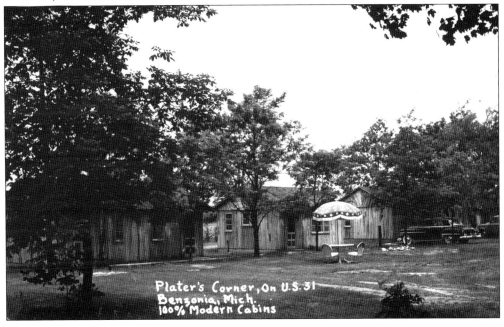
Plater's Corner, On U.S. 31, Benzonia, Mich. 100% Modern Cabins

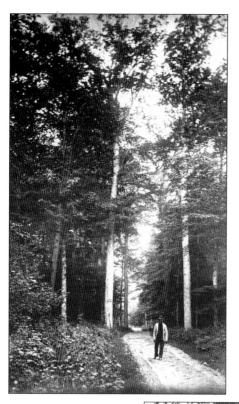

Heading west out of Benzonia is the Frankfort Road, now River Road, which in this photograph from 1889 shows the old growth forest that proved so valuable to the lumber-based economy of the late 19th and early 20th centuries. By 1910, the lumber was largely played out and new means to make a living had to be found, tourism chief among them.

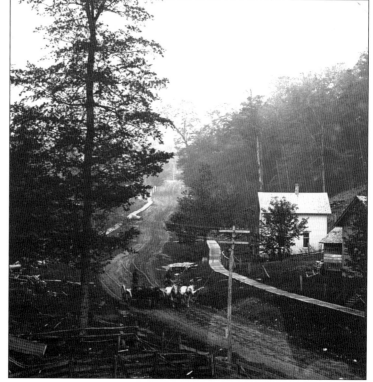

Heading north out of Benzonia and just down the hill, two teamsters plod down Spring Valley Street to Crystal City around 1890. Crystal City and Beulah Resort was the up-and-coming resort town of Crystal Lake. While the roads would remain unimproved for several more decades, locomotives and steamships would transport scores of midwesterners to the new water wonderland.

Two

BEULAH

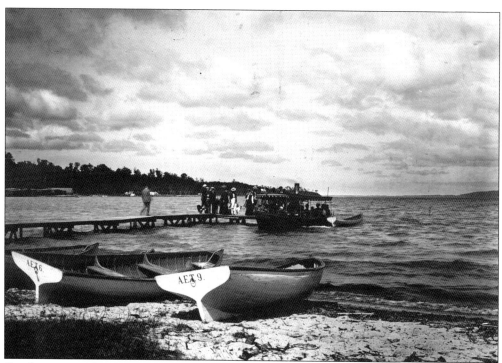

On the eastern shore of Crystal Lake lies Beulah. When the lake was lowered in 1873, sandy beaches were revealed, replacing sheer drop-offs and swamps. With the arrival of the railroad in 1887, the potential for resort development around the lake was realized. The Reverend Charles E. Bailey, founder of Benzonia, purchased the lowland along the eastern lakeshore from the government, drawing criticism for land speculation. Bailey built the first house in his Crystal City and Beulah Resort. The only village directly on Crystal Lake, the community that came to be known as Beulah was the destination for tourists arriving from Toledo, Detroit, Chicago, and St. Louis. At Terpening's Boat Livery, personal crafts or a gas-powered launch such as the *Outing* connected passengers to points around the lake.

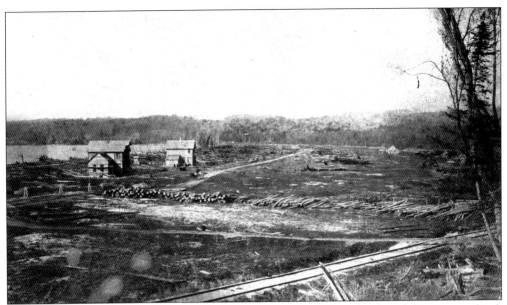

The earliest pictures from what is now Beulah show how it was developed from swampland. The earliest pioneers in the area reported that a man could not walk around the lake without getting his feet wet due to there being no beaches or dry land at the base of the hilly, oval bowl that had Crystal Lake at its center. Because of this, and because there was no river or channel connecting the lake to Lake Michigan, no lumber mill or town was built on its shores. Only after the lake was lowered and the railroad arrived did the full potential of the former lowland become apparent. In photographs from around 1890, the station for Crystal City is pictured, as are several structures on the newly clear-cut fields.

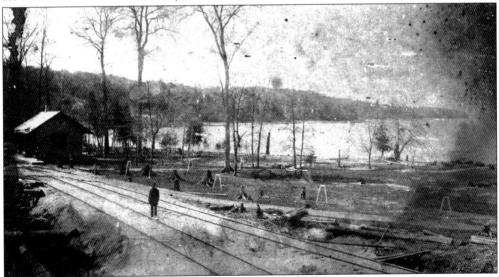

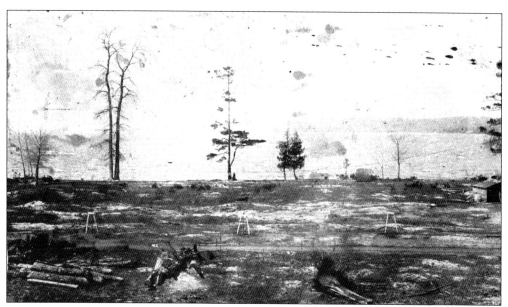

The story of the lowering of Crystal Lake comes from William L. Case, an original settler, preeminent citizen, and businessman. In Case's *The Tragedy of Crystal Lake,* to reap the economic benefits of access to Lake Michigan from Crystal Lake, Archibald Jones sold stock in a company that would build a channel between the two lakes via the Betsie River. A proper survey was never taken and a qualified engineer never consulted to evaluate the plan. When the channel was opened, between 20 and 30 feet of water rushed from Crystal Lake and flooded the Betsie River valley. While a tragedy for those who lost livestock and suffered disruption, the new land opened up Crystal Lake to a new town, summer camps, cottages, and resorts.

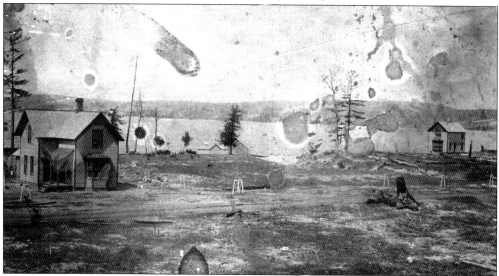

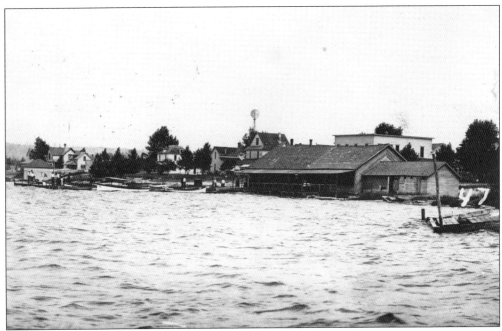

In contrast to Benzonia, Beulah developed as a resort town. What may have been frowned upon in Benzonia was fair game just a few yards down the road at Terpening's Pavilion and Boat Livery, commonly referred to as Terp's. Built around 1900 by Archibald Ethelbert Terpening to service the new resort industry, one could even buy tobacco and cigarettes down at Terp's. Terpening provided a wide range of summer entertainment, including dances every night except Sunday, two well-used bowling alleys, a soda fountain, slot machines, gymnasium equipment, and eventually a hand-cranked movie projector. Besides being the center for amusement, as it was for the toughs posing on Terp's dock, it also served as the gymnasium for the high school for several years in the 1920s.

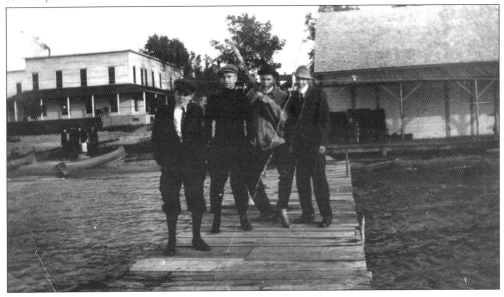

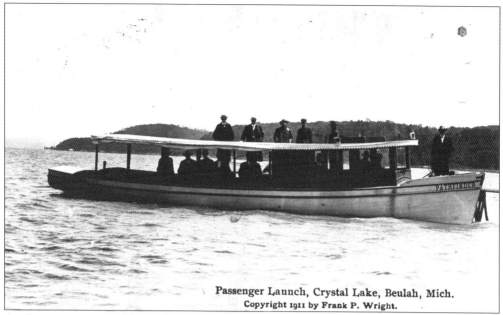

Passenger Launch, Crystal Lake, Beulah, Mich.
Copyright 1911 by Frank P. Wright.

As there were no passable roads around the lake, and the railroad only ran along the southeast corner, the standard mode of transportation for luggage, groceries, building materials, and people was by boat. Finding opportunity in this, Terp's provided three gasoline launches with canopy tops, curtains, and a self-written certificate of operation posted near the steering wheel, the fastest being the *Pathfinder* (above) and the others the *Frances* and the *Tramp*. At the west end of the lake the Congregational Summer Assembly offered its launch, the *Mary Louise* (below). While there are no accounts of a launch disaster ever occurring, no tales from this time on Crystal Lake are complete without the story of a sudden gale catching the steersman by surprise and frightening passengers in the middle of a crossing.

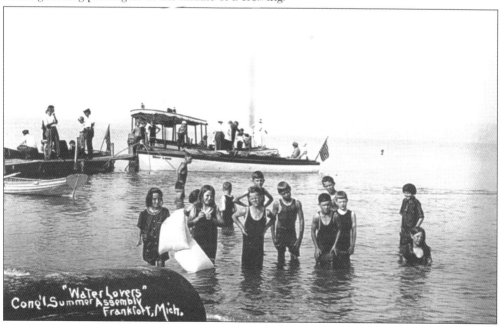

"Water Lovers"
Cong'l Summer Assembly
Frankfort, Mich.

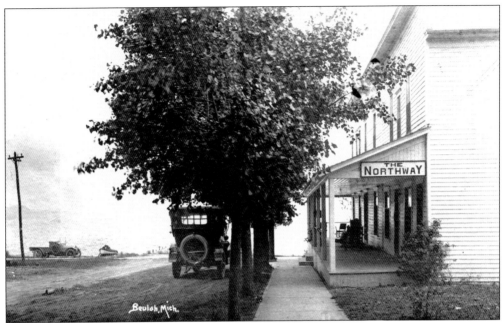

Just to the north of Terp's was one of the more commodious hotels on Crystal Lake, the Northway. Originally built as a boardinghouse for salesmen in the 1890s by Tom White, White's Hotel was sold to Frank Orcutt, who changed its name to the Crystal Inn. Dr. Peter Northway, who came from Owosso to play clarinet at Terp's, met Orcutt's daughter Nancy at a dance and married her in 1911.

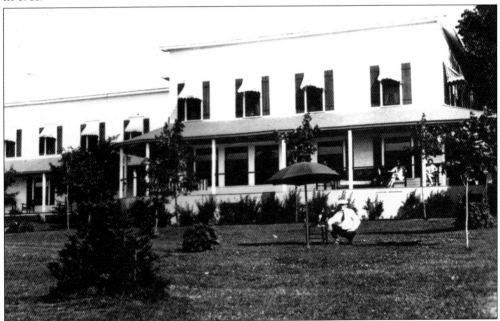

Peter Northway had a third interest in the hotel, and it was decided to change its name to the Northway. In a picture from the 1920s, Frank Orcutt poses with his dog Tiger on the Northway's lawn, which stretched to the beach. The beauty of the site lent itself to events, such as Benzonia's graduation ceremonies.

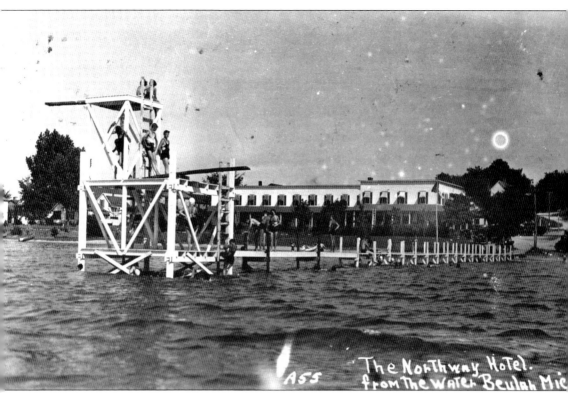

With its long dock and access to a diving platform, the Northway became the center of attention for vacationers in Beulah. Over the summer months the Northway Hotel and restaurant provided jobs for the area's teenagers. The boys working at the hotel could afford the gentleman's dime entry fee for the evening dances next door at Terp's.

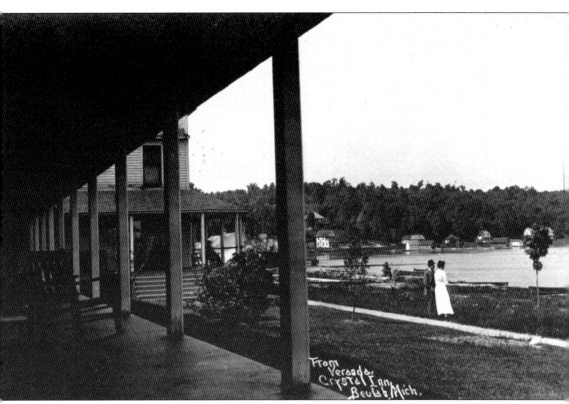

A view from the veranda of the Northway sometime before 1911, when it was still known as the Crystal Inn, shows the new cottages being built around the lake near Beulah. Terpening's Pavilion and Boat Livery, just out of sight behind the porch, would be a convenient stroll to the left for the couple in the picture.

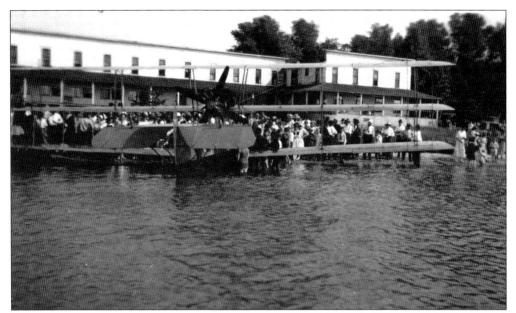

Sometimes a big event would occur on Beulah Beach, putting the Northway Hotel at the center of things. When a triple-winged flying boat arrived on the lake sometime after World War I, curious residents swarmed the beach. Those lucky enough to have the money could even be taken for a ride. This same plane is shown on postcards at a beach on the west end of the lake, near the Congregational Summer Assembly, with similar swarms of people.

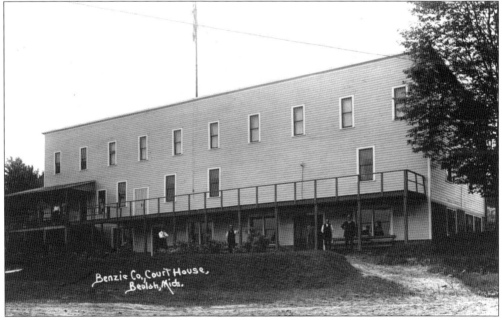

Providing brief competition for Terp's was the Grand, built in 1912. It was intended as an amusement center, and owners Thomas Toland and Gilbert Nisewander had installed billiard tables, bowling alleys, an ice-cream parlor, and slot machines. The second floor was given to meetings and dances. In 1916, Beulah was chosen as the county seat, and the Grand was purchased and used as the county courthouse until the 1970s.

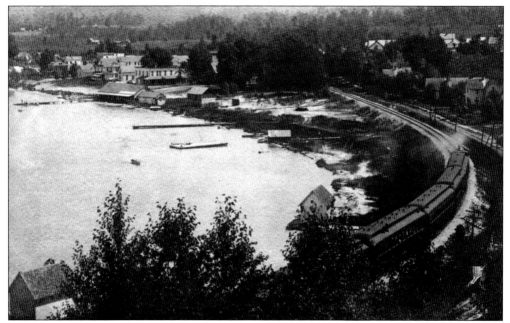

Terp's and the Northway Hotel (above, left background) are seen as a summer-length passenger train makes its way along the shoreline. Originally Crystal City was the name for Benzonia's railroad depot on the lake. However, the Reverend Charles E. Bailey tacked on "Beulah Resort," giving rise to the official name of the village when the depot was built in the 1895, and "Beulah" was spelled out in large, white, capital letters by the Ann Arbor Railroad. The Beulah to which Bailey referred was popular in hymns of the era, Beulahland lying on the border to heaven. Beulah is from older Bible translations of Isaiah 62:4, "but thou shalt be called Hephzibah, and thy land Beulah for Jehovah delighteth in thee, and thy land shall be married."

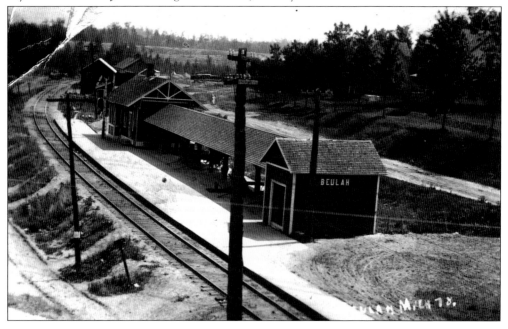

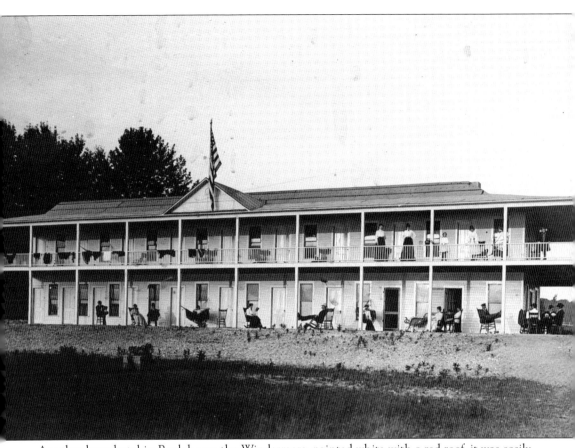

Another large hotel in Beulah was the Windermere; painted white with a red roof, it was easily seen from all points around Crystal Lake. It was originally built in 1903 by O. L. Bristol, the Shiawassee County school commissioner who vacationed on Crystal Lake. He and his wife were able to purchase 80 acres of lake frontage and virgin timber for $800 and then build the hotel from their plot's milled lumber.

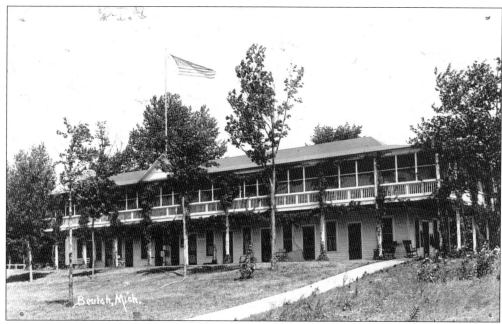

When O. L. Bristol and his wife opened the Windermere, room and board for a week was a competitive $27.50 per guest. Bristol went on the serve as Benzie County school commissioner and the superintendent of Benzonia public schools.

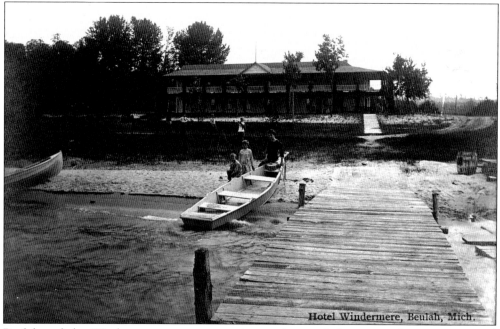

Beulah and the Windermere were no exception to the trend that saw early resorts initiated by religious groups seeking retreat. In 1911, the Bristols sold the hotel to a group of 10 Jewish families from the Cleveland area who converted the hotel to a private club. Some resorts and properties from this time began to publicize their offerings as "restricted."

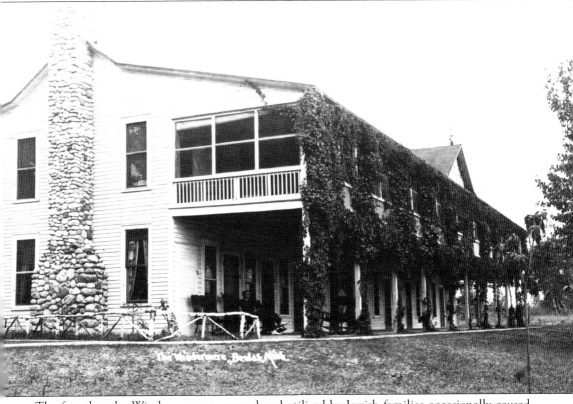

The fact that the Windermere was owned and utilized by Jewish families occasionally caused some consternation for the Christian assemblies and residents around Crystal Lake. Once the pastor of the Benzonia Congregational Church invited a noted rabbi staying at the hotel to speak to his congregation. After some expression of misgivings by the congregants, the program was very well received.

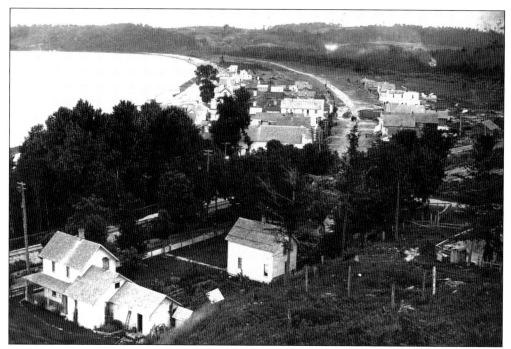

A photograph taken from on top of the hill in Benzonia, around 1900, shows Beulah's Main Street and railroad line (above). After Crystal Lake was lowered, the Reverend Charles E. Bailey named the former swampland he purchased Crystal City and Beulah Resort. Benzonia and this tract of land were formally considered the same municipal entity until the 1930s. With its easier access to the railroad line, its location directly on the lake, and its lax attitude toward alcohol and tobacco, growth in Beulah as a resort town accelerated while Benzonia struggled in its effort to start a college. Despite their proximity, literally a stone's throw away, both settlements would have their own post offices and newspapers. Dr. Powers (below) poses for a picture in front of the Beulah Post Office, with the Ann Arbor depot in the background.

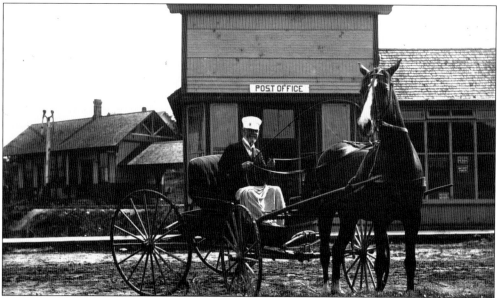

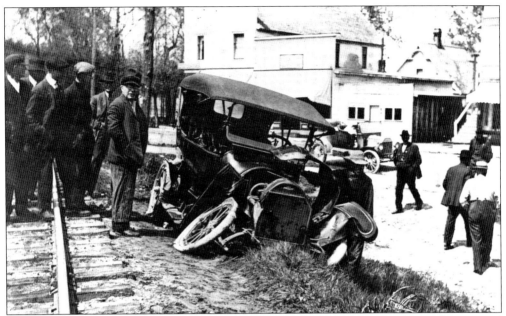

Even though the world moved at a slower pace in 1923, it was getting quicker and trains and automobiles did not always mix well, as seen in a photograph of an unfortunate encounter between the two in Beulah (above). The railroad tracks, after hugging Crystal Lake, cut through the main street with the depot providing a convenient loading dock for the merchants along the street who would transport the merchandise to their stores with a wheelbarrow. The building at the center (below), with the pitch off-center, belonged at the time to Albert and Hattie Knight, pioneers to the area, who operated a grocery and general store in the location from 1904 to 1947.

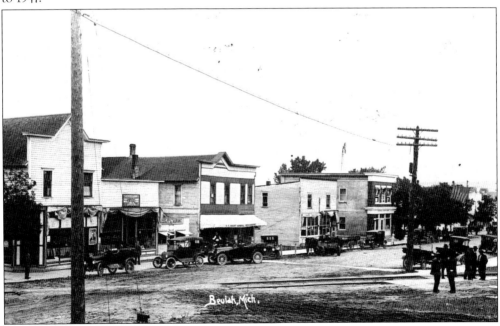

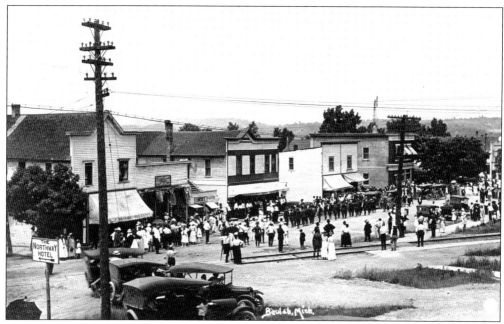

Around the corner from the Northway Hotel and Terp's stood the drugstore owned by John Gibb (above). Gibb was a Muskegon friend of Frank Orcutt, the man who had moved to the area a short time before and bought what would become the Northway. Orcutt encouraged Gibb, a young druggist, to try his luck with a business in the growing town of about 250 people. After traveling up the shore of Lake Michigan in a launch, a feat that he vowed to never repeat, he set himself up in his new business shortly before 1900. He was known for his chocolate sodas, making the chocolate himself, and sales were brisk with the Fourth of July crowds in town (below).

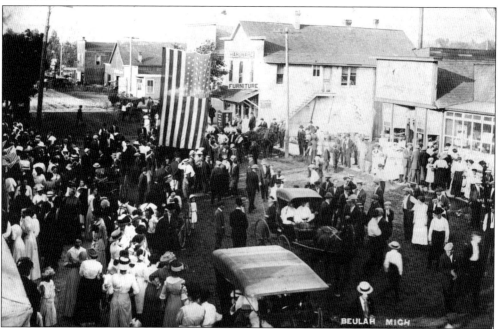

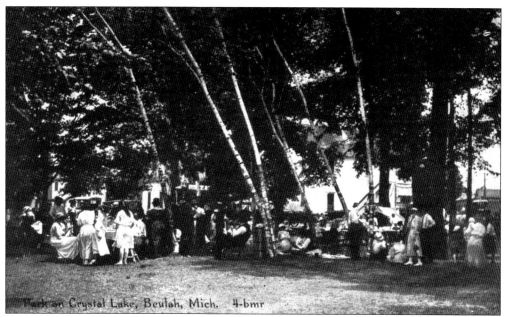

Park on Crystal Lake, Beulah, Mich. 4-bmr

With its miles of shoreline and destinations for boaters, with the picnic sites among its bays and coves and wooded glens, with its inns and restaurants at picturesque locales, with its brooks and springs and cascading streams, and with its shady parks and pavilions and soda fountains, Crystal Lake with Beulah as its headquarters became a vacation destination and the meeting place for those who kept permanent summer homes. With gatherings at Beulah Park on the Fourth of July sometime in the 1920s (above), or at the Mid-Summer Resort Carnival next door at Crystal Beach in the 1930s (below), the east shore bustled as the center of activity.

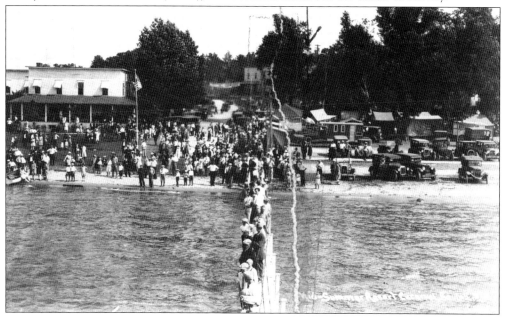

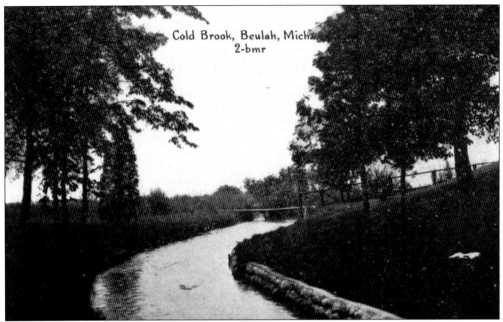

With no major river emptying into Crystal Lake, and outside of the natural springs, the only source of freshwater running into Crystal Lake is Cold Creek (above), pictured on a quiet summer day. This compares to the crowds attending the early spring smelt run on Cold Creek (below). When the water warms to 42 degrees in March, the smelt start running. Until smelt dipping was regulated by the state, thousands would come to Beulah's Cold Creek every spring to scoop out the silvery fish by the net full. It was reported in the 1930s that 20,000 men, women, and children dipped a ton of smelt a day for over a week. Local restaurants and motels would be open 24 hours a day to take advantage of the yearly boom.

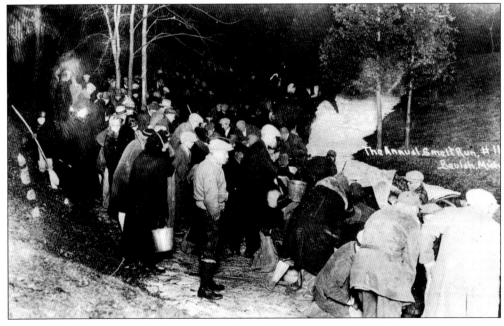

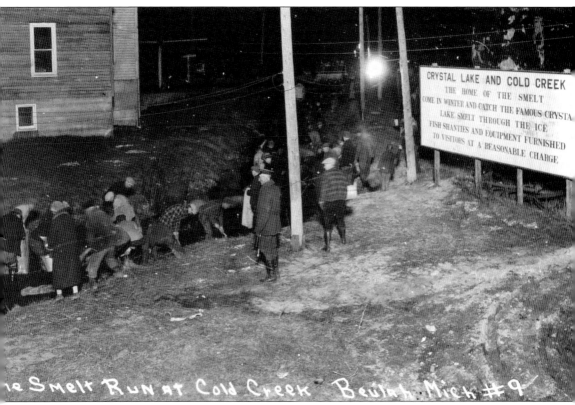

Transplanted from Maine in 1912, smelt were intended to feed the landlocked salmon that had been stocked in Crystal Lake. The salmon soon died out, but the smelt thrived. In the 1920s, word began to spread of the sport and good eating. As smelt are seldom seen and run only at night, thousands of people came to line the banks of Cold Creek at dark, waiting behind a rope cordon for the start of the cold spring ritual.

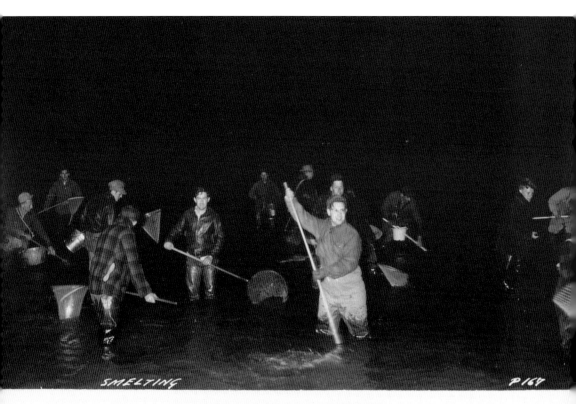

Greetings from Beulah, Michigan

When the stream was packed with smelt, a gun was fired and floodlights strung along the creek were switched on. The cordon dropped, and as state troopers climbed trees and jumped onto fence posts to get out of the way, the mass of dippers descended into the creek. After an hour or so the dipping ended, and the people retreated again to the rope cordons to wait in the dark. About an hour before dawn, after the stream had filled with smelt, the action was repeated. On several occasions between 1927 and 1931, the governor of Michigan, Fred W. Green, was even on hand to flip the light switch.

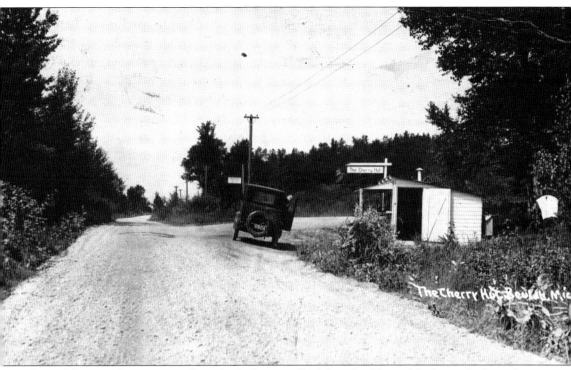

One of the most famous stops along the highway in Beulah is the Cherry Hut begun by James L. and Dorothy Kraker. This 1922 photograph shows the original pie stand along the north shore, made from a chicken coop and where the pies were baked on top of a kerosene stove.

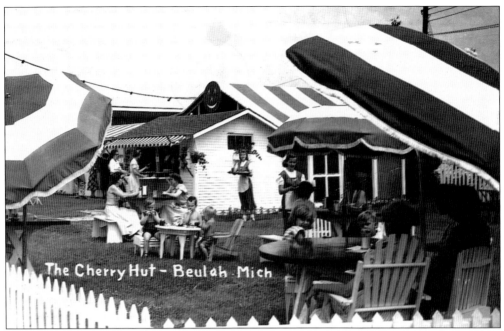

The Krakers soon added a pavilion at their stand so that the customers could sit and enjoy their pie in a picturesque location. With their success they opened a second shop in Benzonia in 1928. In 1935, they moved all their operations to Beulah, where the business continued to grow. The symbol of the smiling face cut into their crusts, Cherry Jerry, greeted the motorists as they stopped for their treat.

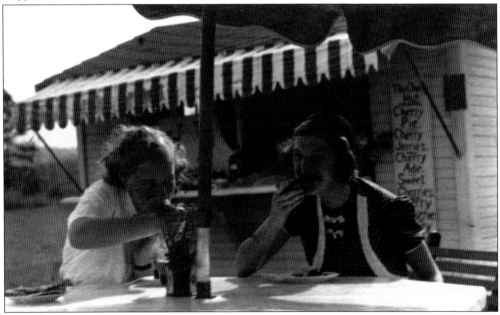

The frozen pie business expanded under the name of Pet-Ritz pies and was eventually bought by Pet Foods. In 1959, the Cherry Hut restaurant and jam business was bought by Leonard Case, who had started as a young man working at the jam store in Benzonia. In this picture, two patrons from the Crystalaire Camp for Girls enjoy their wedge of pie in 1942.

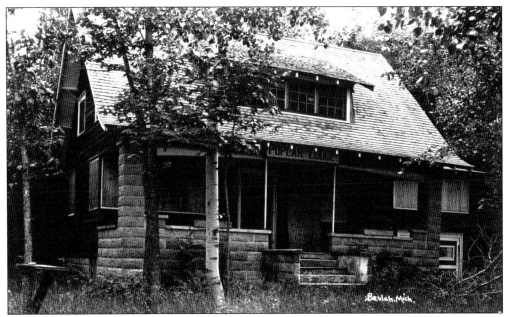

As the season drew to a close in fall, fewer excursions were made by the railroads and traffic along the highway and around the lake lightened. Many of the cottages, hotels, and lodges dotting the lakeshore were boarded up for the winter months and left to the care of those who checked up on them from time to time.

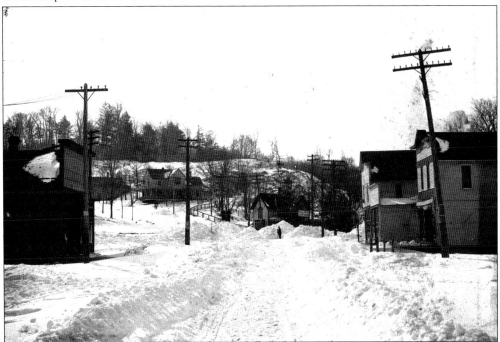

A Beulah street scene from about 1915 shows the change of the seasons. Winter would come, and the drugstores and groceries and soda fountains would quiet. The dances and plays were moved into the churches and halls for those who ventured out on foot or sleigh to brave the steep hills and the snow as it piled higher and higher.

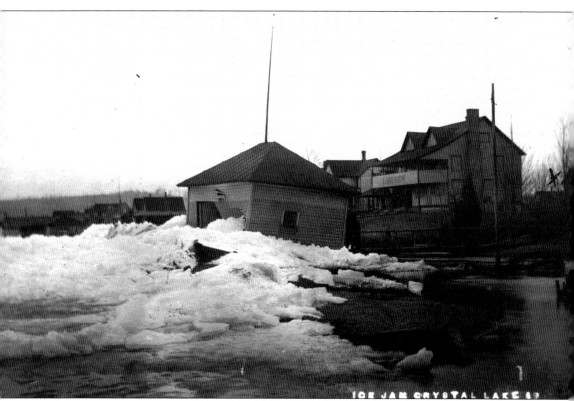

As the cold winds blew, the ice on Crystal Lake shifted and sometimes damaged buildings placed on the beach for warmer times, as was this boathouse. During thaws, ice jams would block Cold Creek from emptying into the lake. By opening day, however, the repairs were made and all was ready for another season.

Three
COTTAGES, RESORTS, AND CAMPS

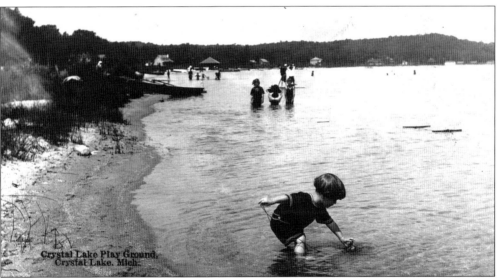

As the waters from the accidental lowering of Crystal Lake receded in 1873, swampy land drained, beaches appeared, and with improved transportation by ship and rail, vacationers began to flock to Lake Michigan and Crystal Lake for the cool summer breezes in the time before air-conditioning. Some could afford to own and maintain their own cottages while others rented. Before the automobile, camping in the woods or along the rivers and lakes was generally done by children at the summer camps and those who came to the area to ride on horseback along the beaches. Those of like mind in religion staked out their sections around the lake as Jews gathered at the Windermere in Beulah on the east shore, the Congregationalists at Pilgrim on the west shore, and the Disciples of Christ along the south shore. However, no matter the philosophy or denomination, Crystal Lake had become a playground for those with the means to travel and spend a week or a summer in God's country.

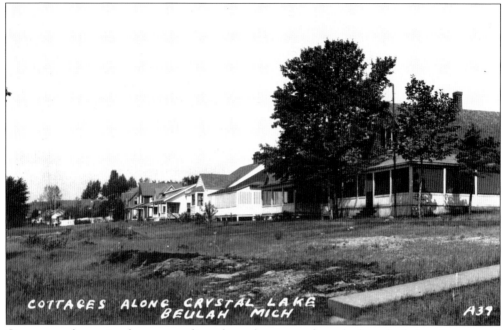

Cottages and vacation homes standing along the east and north shore had the advantage of being built directly on the beach (above), while those built along the south shore, at least for a mile or so, had the Ann Arbor Railroad train track and the road between them and the beach (below). After spending a day bathing in the cool lake waters, the screen porches allowed the cottagers to spend their nights outside on the sleeping porch. Breathing the healthy air with the fresh lake breeze was an important draw for the area at a time when many still believed that unhealthy air was the cause of many diseases.

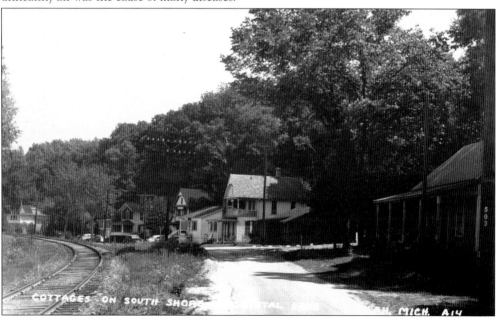

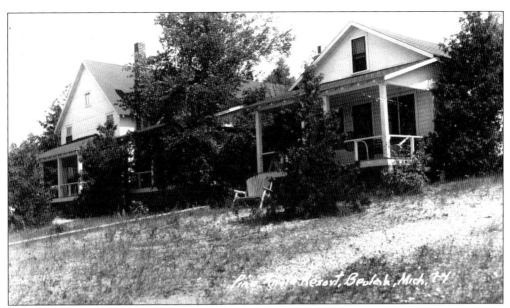

When the automobile became a common form of transportation for all classes of people, a new type of resort opened up along the highways to Crystal Lake and along its shores. Pine Knote Resort (above) and Rice's Service and Cabins (below) were examples of conveniently accessible vacation rentals for motorists. Begun in the 1920s, resorts with small cabins and bungalows catered to the rising middle-class factory workers who could afford the cars they were making and had vacation time. Likewise, around the lakes and on the rivers flowing into them, campgrounds were created by people who otherwise had no use for the too sandy or swampy soil, offering easy access for the fishing and boating.

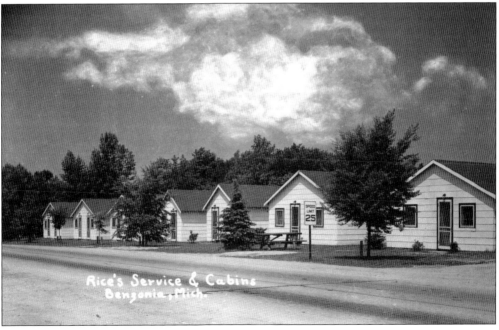

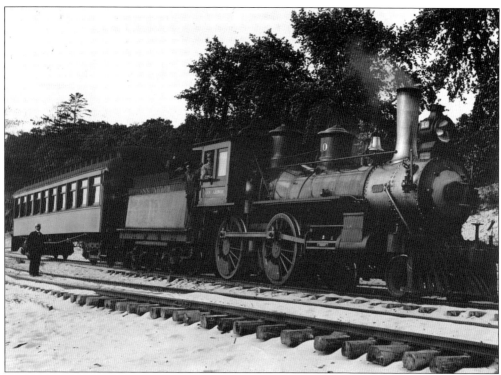

The "Ping Pong" train (above) was operated by the Ann Arbor Railroad to provide service between Beulah and its Royal Frontenac Hotel in Frankfort. It was called the Ping Pong because, with no turnaround for the train, the engine with its one or two passenger cars would run forward to Beulah and backward to Frankfort several times a day. Those who chose a resort, hotel, or cottage on the southeast shore of the lake had an easy and convenient mode of transportation as it would drop off and pick up passengers along the way at flag stations. For those who had cottages on the beach along the north shore (below), transportation needed to be arranged out of Beulah.

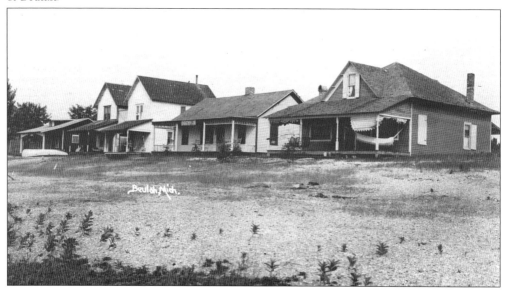

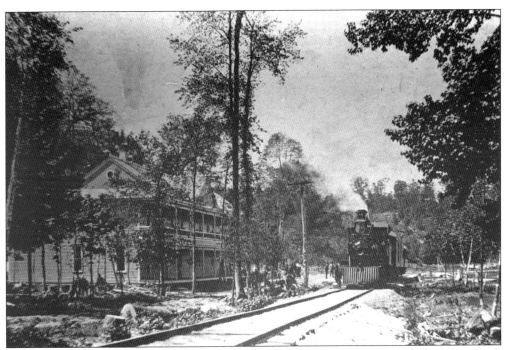

The last flag stop for the Ping Pong train heading east was the Van Winkle Hotel in Beulah (above), where vacationers could relax on rocking chairs and swing in hammocks along the long porch (below). Built by Louis Van Winkle at the urging of the Ann Arbor Railroad, it was in operation from 1890 until Van Winkle lost it in the panic of 1895; a short time later it burned down. Until the middle of the 20th century, the resort season generally lasted only from the Fourth of July to the end of August. Since hotel owners had only a few short weeks to make expenses and earn a living, it was not uncommon to hear of hotels and resort buildings burning over the winter months. When this happened, whispers of "insurance money" were heard in the churches, dance halls, and saloons.

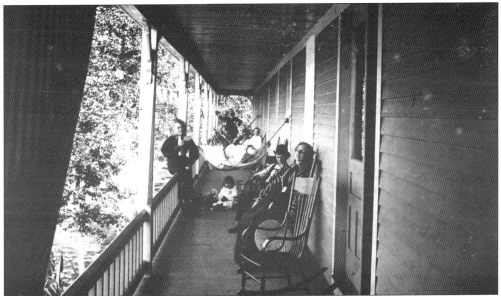

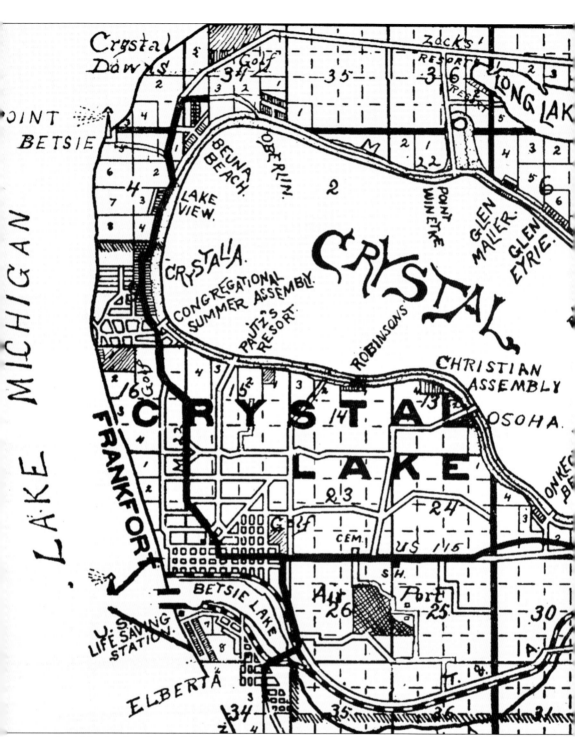

A widely circulated map of Crystal Lake shows the developed resorts, assemblies, and camps along the south, east, and west shores and the subdivisions and family compounds along the north shore. Round Lake, unlabeled but included just to the southwest of Long Lake, was originally a part of Crystal Lake until its lowering in 1873; the shaded region between the two lakes indicates

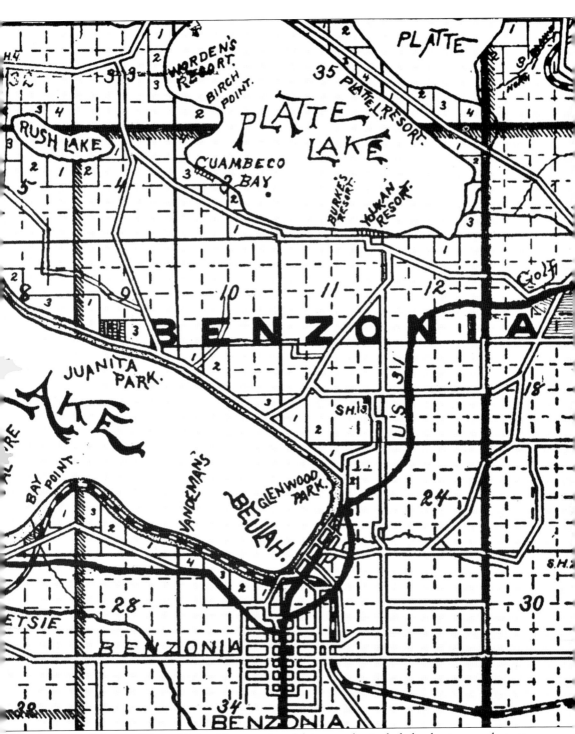

the original shape of Crystal Lake. Many copies of this map also included a short poem that ran in place of the "Crystal Lake" lettering, which read, "The place we fish and pass the dish and loiter in the wood, Now you must come and bring your chum and ramble to the good."

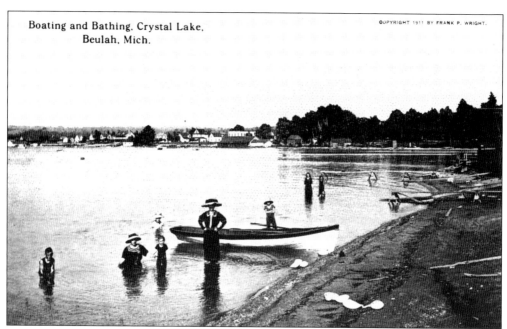

On postcards and in letters from the time, women bathed rather than swam. The heavy woolen bathing suits and broad hats worn by these women made it impossible for them to do more than wade and take a dip. In the far background is Terp's and behind that the Northway Hotel.

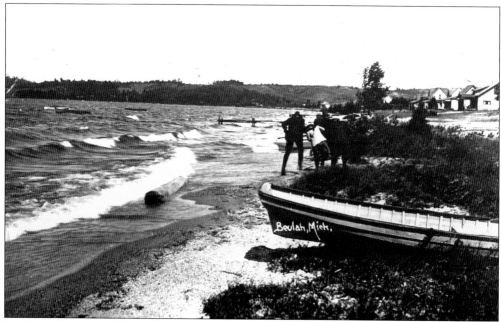

On the earliest maps, Crystal Lake was named Cap Lake, some say due to the white caps created by the dominant winds from Lake Michigan and the lake's northwest to southeast axis. Walking along the beach on a blustery day could prove a difficult task with the northwest wind blowing over the nine-mile open expanse of the lake.

Jacob Seel, in about 1910, is seen standing among his trees at the J. J. Seel Orchard, which occupied over 1,500 feet of frontage on Crystal Lake. In the winter, the moderating temperatures and humidity of Lake Michigan made the shoreline an ideal region for cherries, peaches, and apples. In the lower areas on the east shore, celery and onions were produced at the Trapp farm.

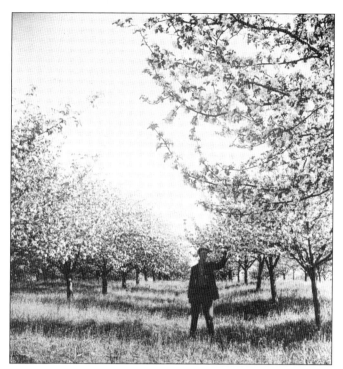

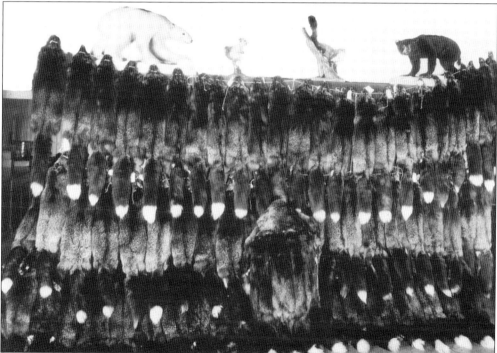

A unique sort of farming took place along the eastern shore—raising foxes. Started in 1922, Justus E. Smith and his Crystal Silver Fox Ranch were raising over 1,100 foxes, producing fox pelts for fashionable ladies until 1939 when longhair fur went out of fashion. The pelting took place in November or December, when the year's harvest was displayed.

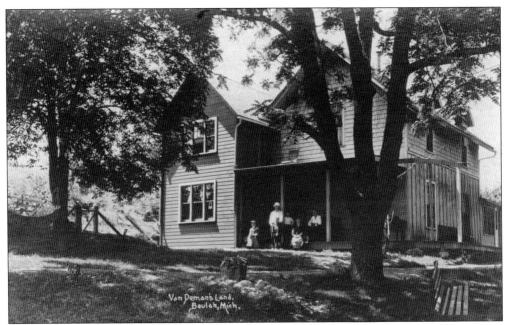

The resort nearest Beulah that had the privilege of being a flag station by the Ann Arbor Railroad's Ping Pong train was Van Deman's land, the tracks running just to the north of the compound between the resort and the lake. The railroad's inexpensive excursions led J. W. Van Deman, a veteran of the Grand Army of the Republic who had been wounded in the toe, to develop his piece of property running along the lake. The resort's growth happened sporadically and piecemeal. At first, vacationers came simply to fish. Then they stayed a little longer and set up camp. Finally Van Deman and his regulars began to build cabins here and there to accommodate the yearly influx.

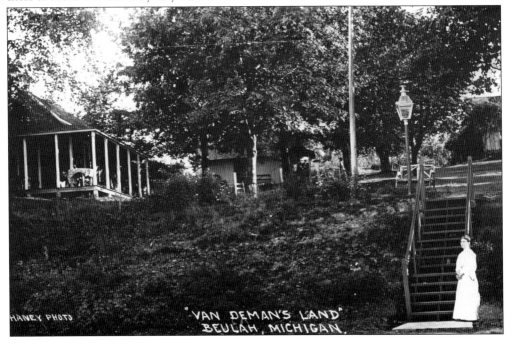

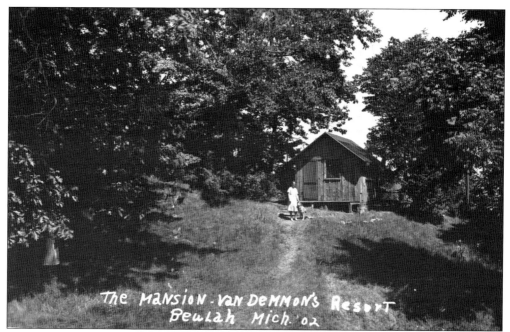

The Mansion - Van Demmon's Resort Beulah Mich. '02

At its height, between 40 and 50 resorters kept Van Deman's at its capacity throughout the summer season. Because of its unique development, it was run a bit differently than many of the other resorts dotting the lake. As there was no central hotel building, and as all the guests were lodged in separate small cabins, their meals were served at a central dining hall with the food coming from the Van Deman farm. When the resort was sold, it was renamed Hill and Dale and operated through the 1970s.

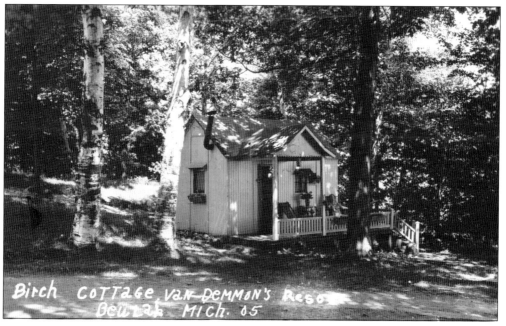

Birch Cottage, Van Demmon's Resort Beulah Mich. 05

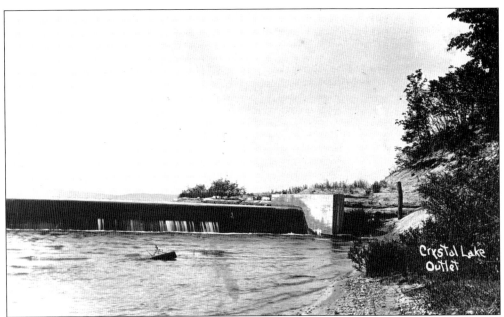

The level of Crystal Lake is maintained at the outlet along the south shore, near Bay Point. For a time, Bay Point Lodge at Crystal Camp for Boys hosted lucky boys from the Chicago area in the 1930s through the generosity of Charles Ward Seabury, a Chicago insurance businessman and philanthropist. The Seaburys had been resorting on Crystal Lake since 1917 and eventually would build a compound of their own on the north shore. The porch of the lodge for the boys' camp, which wrapped around the building, was full of Ping Pong tables and various activities for the campers.

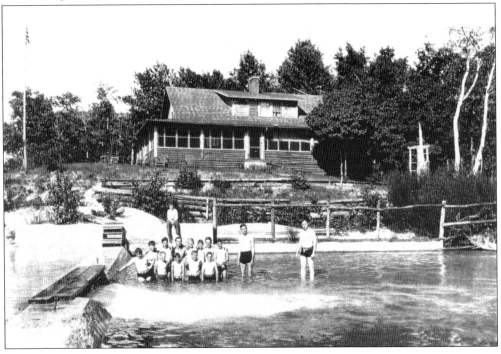

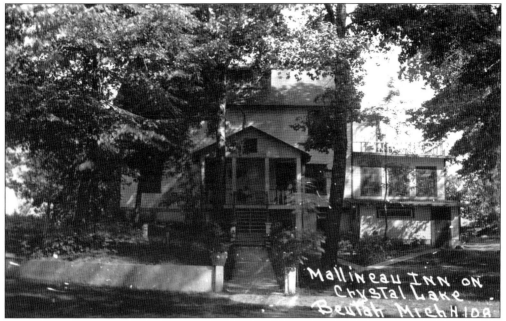

The Mollineaux Inn, built in 1911 by M. Mollineaux, had a reputation for its chicken and fish dinners and advertised itself as "overlooking clear blue waters which rival Switzerland's Lake Geneva in scenic charm." It spanned along the peninsula to Bay Point with a string of cottages. It also had the privilege of being a flag stop for the Ping Pong train between Frankfort and Beulah, which assured it easy access for its many visitors from Chicago and St. Louis. The lobby from about 1945 (below) shows the grand fireplace with the unique feature of a Native American head and horseshoe in its stonework.

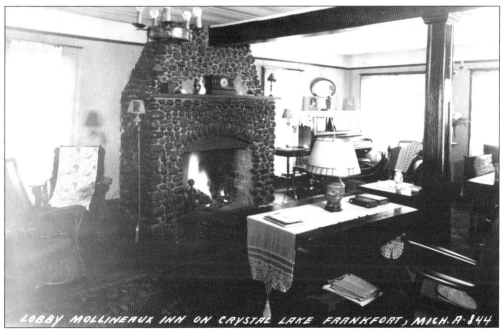

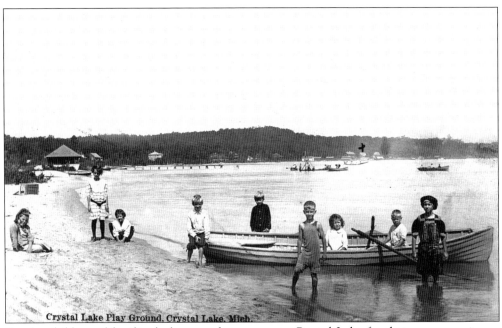
Crystal Lake Play Ground, Crystal Lake, Mich.

For the children of families lucky enough to come to Crystal Lake for their summers, it was usually a time spent without their fathers. Most often businessmen from the larger cities, the men sent their families without them in the early summer, having already made arrangements for a resort or cottage rental. If they did travel with their families, they usually returned to home and work after their wives and children were settled in their summer paradise, coming later in the summer for their two- or three-week vacation. For young people, summer acquaintances turned into summer romances at the many dances, tennis matches, and outings. Most honored would be the young lady's beau from home, invited to spend some time at her family's cottage.

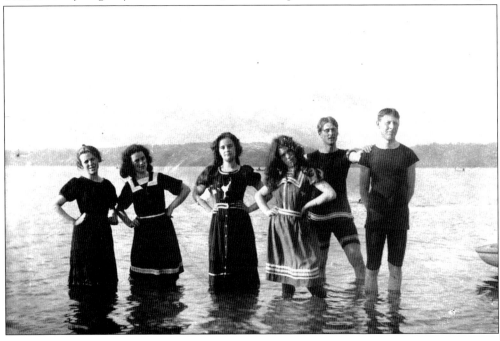

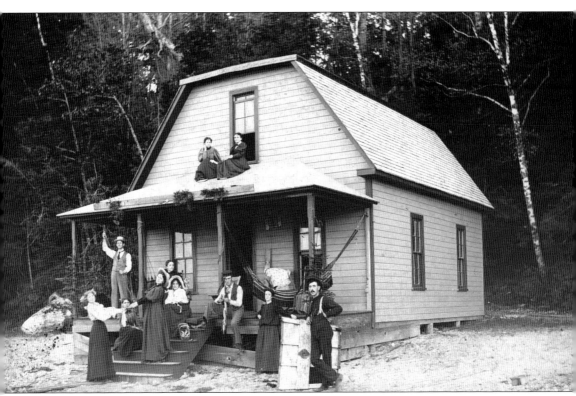

A photograph from 1895 shows a camping party at the Robinson Resort along the south shore of the lake. One of the oldest and most publicized resorts, Robinson's was started in 1891 when George R. Robinson arrived from Olivet. Olivet was a city centered around a Congregational college much like Benzonia sought to be, and the reputation of the Crystal Lake area was becoming well known among Congregationalists in the Midwest.

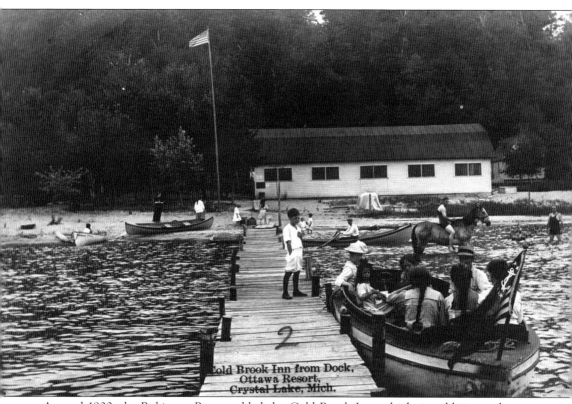
Around 1900, the Robinson Resort added the Cold Brook Inn, which, in addition to being a place to catch a launch, became a destination for those seeking restaurant or fountain service.

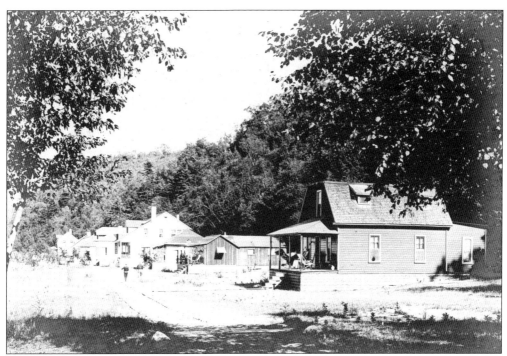

Robinson began to sell lots on his property about the same time as the steamships and railroads started bringing tourists to the area. By 1923, 30 cottages had been built at the resort. A central dining hall was provided for those who did not want to prepare their own meals at their cottages. Tennis courts, hiking trails, and croquet grounds spanned the 65-acre compound, which included a "Robin Hood archery roving course" in a "Sherwood Forest setting." In addition to easy access to boating, fishing, and bathing, families could participate in organized, supervised sports. Like Van Deman's farther west, Robinson's farm produced the food used at his dining hall and inn.

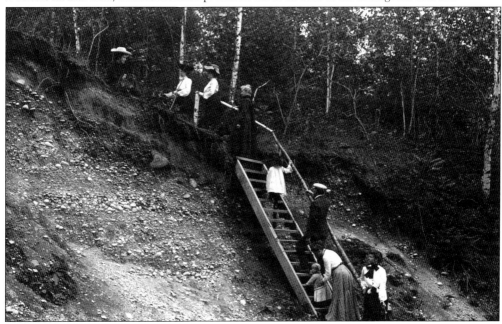

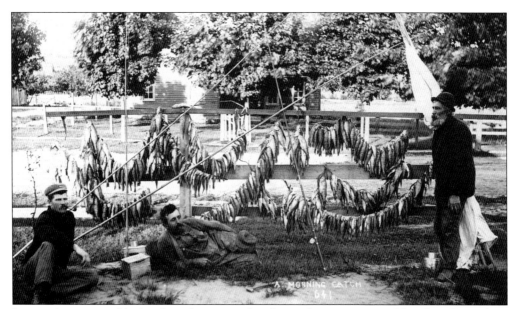

It was often repeated by locals and in tourist brochures that a person could pull in 60 perch in an hour on Crystal Lake, as illustrated by some men displaying their morning catch at the resort (above). Built on a gentle slope going into the lake, Robinson's bragged that the sandy, sloping beach was safe and it never had a drowning. Open April 1 through November 15, it touted that "our fall is ideal for hay fever sufferers." Like most of the resorts around the lake, table settings and boat rentals were included in the fee, and bed linens could be furnished at an additional fee for those who did not want to bring them from home. The landmark Cold Brook Inn was torn down in 1975.

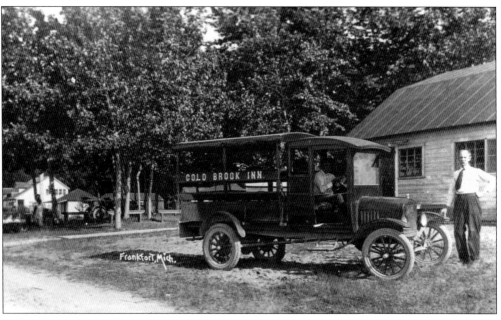

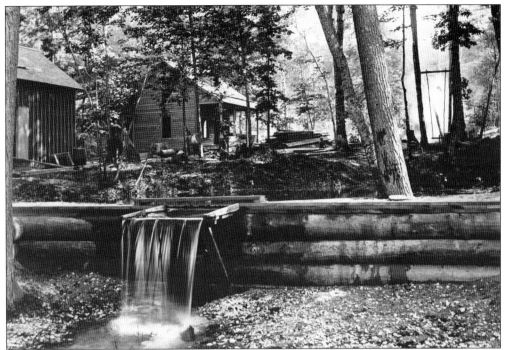

The first resort on Crystal Lake was Crystal Banks, begun by A. E. Banks. With the arrival of the railroads, he built several cottages and a pier and then sold the concern in 1891 to Robert Pautz, who had acquired the funds after winning the Irish sweepstakes. His daughter, Edith, had lent him $1 from her teacher's salary to play.

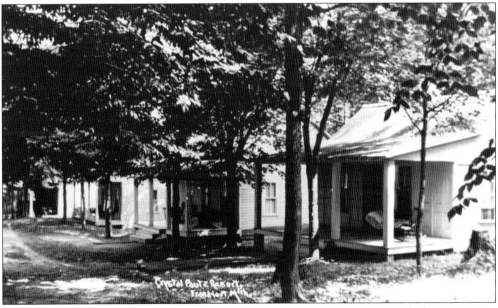

Pautz changed the name to Crystal Pautz Resort, and by the 1920s, it consisted of nine cottages and a lodge, built on a swath of land stretching southward along a stream for a quarter mile. The cabins came completely equipped, except for linens and silverware. In advertising, it was assured that "swimming in Crystal Lake's crystal clear water gives you a thrill long to be remembered."

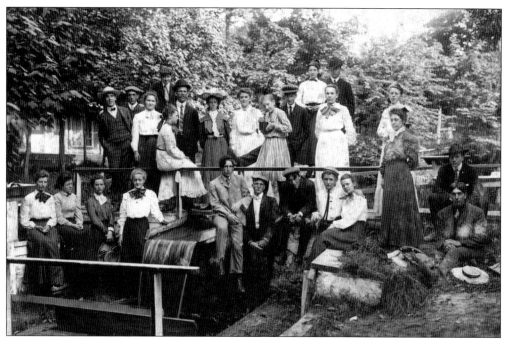

In addition to giving paying guests access to the amenities provided by the resort, the Pautzes were happy to have local residents come to the resort's park and picnic area to enjoy a summer's day. A group identified as coming from Benzonia, probably from the Benzonia Academy, participates in such an outing at the resort in 1911.

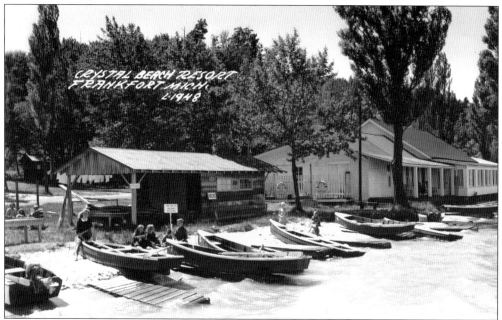

As with most resorts on the lake, boats could be rented from the livery at Pautz's. After spending a day swimming and playing around the resort, children with money could also buy some ice cream for a nickel at the kiosk, although the sign near the boats warns them "Don't Step on Rollers You'll Fall."

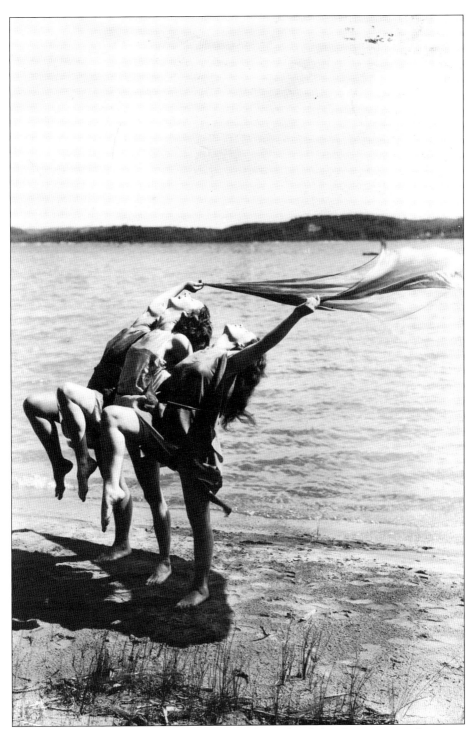

In the early 1920s, Elizabeth Dudley Mattson, the wife of the Congregational minister in Manistee, rented the Mills Community House in Benzonia for two months each summer as a camp for girls. Named Osaha-of-the-Dunes, one of the purposes of the camp was "to develop the integrity of character that leads to a realization of the finest womanhood."

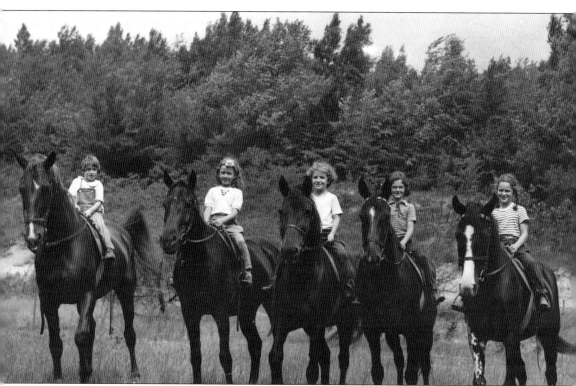

In spite of operating with very little capital, 600 feet of frontage was purchased on Crystal Lake to establish Osaha-of-the-Dunes, and by 1925, a 20-page brochure was produced. The fee for the full summer (eight weeks) was $200, and $115 for half the season. For horseback riding, a popular activity, $35 assured 24 one-hour rides.

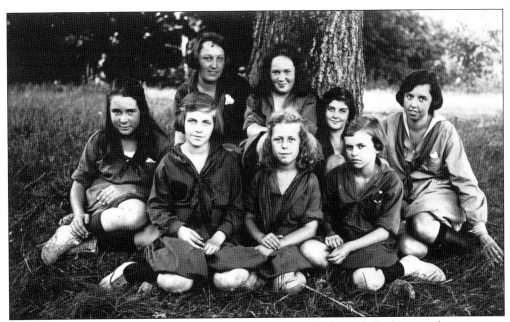

In the earlier years of the camp, life was regimented and the girls had to purchase a camp uniform from Marshall Field's in Chicago of a khaki middy and bloomers with a dark green tie. By the mid-1930s, the camp was open to 50 girls and cost $325 for the summer. A uniform was no longer required, but the girls were expected to wear white on Sundays. Like most camps in the area, participation was limited to member families and those known personally by the director, and as children grew up and out of camp, member families would recommend another family's children to take the open spots.

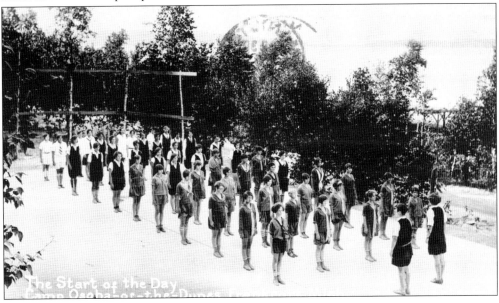

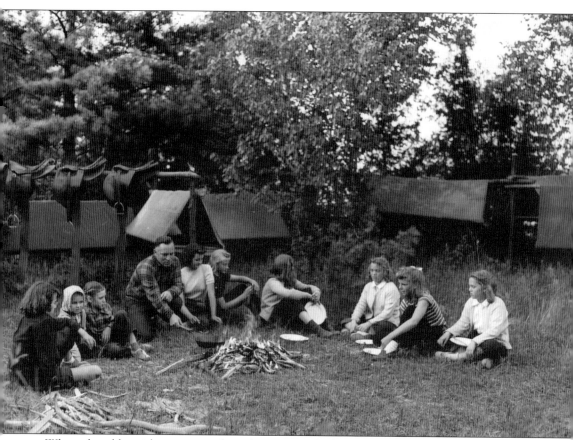

When the older girls participated in their overnight horseback ride and camping trip, they erected their famous "swingwams" for shelter. It was noted by camp participants that if they were caught in the rain, it was more important to shelter the expensive leather saddles as the girls were more quickly dried off with less damage.

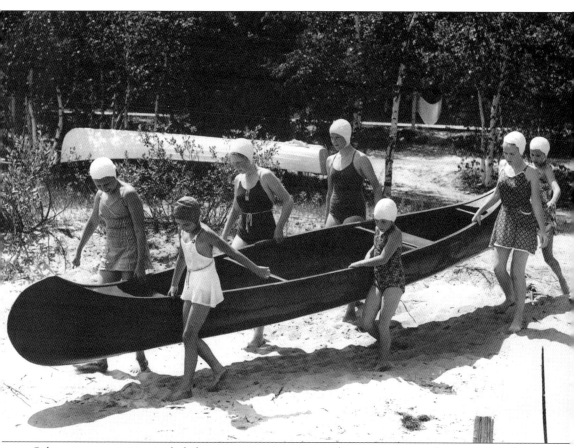

Other camp activities included water sports, canoeing, theater, puppetry, dance, and crafts. A camp bell was rung every hour to signal the change of activity. For several years, a noted geologist and botanist from Northwestern University, Dr. W. G. Waterman, led field trips among the dunes that left a lasting impression on the girls.

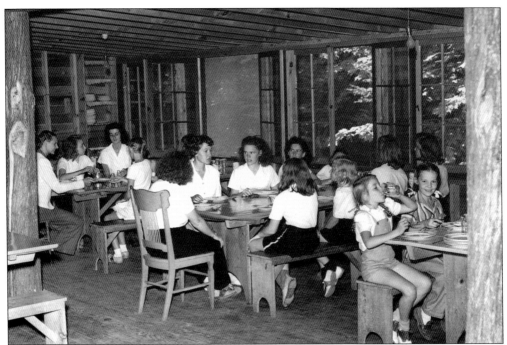

In the 1940s, Osaha-of-the-Dunes was sold to Dr. and Mrs. Fenimore Putt, who changed the name to Crystalaire Camp for Girls. Affectionately known as "Ma and Pop Putt," they invested their time and money in repairing the older buildings and improving the physical plant. Around and down well-shaded paths from the lodge where meals were taken (above) were the cabins, which received names such as Chipmunk and Mousetrap (below). Dr. Putt practiced dentistry in Grosse Pointe and recruited clientele from the Detroit area and Shaker Heights in Ohio. The camp attracted the daughters of prominent citizens and industrialists and was advertised in magazines such as *Good Housekeeping*. In the 1970s, it became a coed camp and was in operation until 2007.

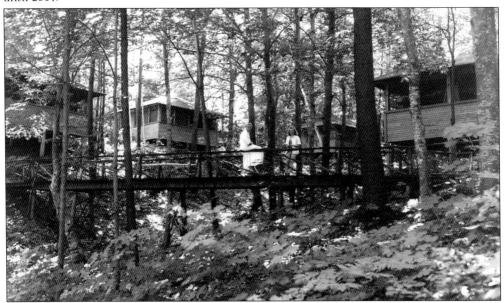

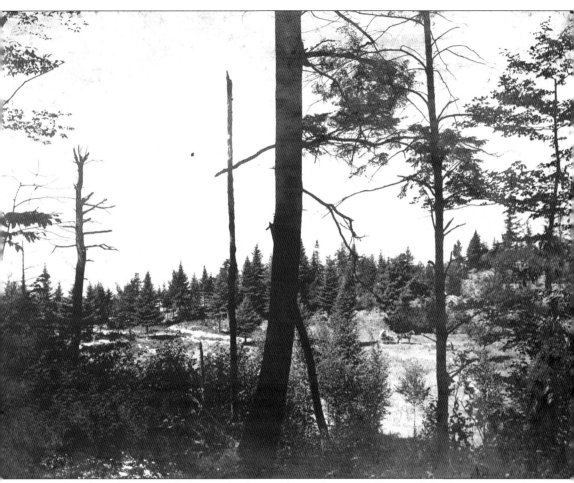

Extending from the west end of Crystal Lake to Lake Michigan is Pilgrim and the Congregational Summer Assembly, with a commanding view of the Big Lake. It was begun by the Cleveland Congregational Conference as a summer resort with Bible study as a central feature. The Ann Arbor Railroad offered the original land to the assembly in 1904 on condition that improvements be made on the property within five years.

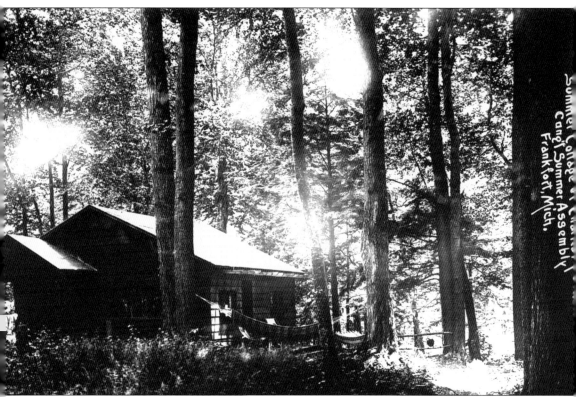

After the terms of agreement between the Congregational Summer Assembly and the Ann Arbor Railroad were met, the assembly went on to purchase more land around Crystal Lake. Early participants with means bought their property and built their cabins, such as Charles M. Sheldon, with his hammocks strung among the tall trees.

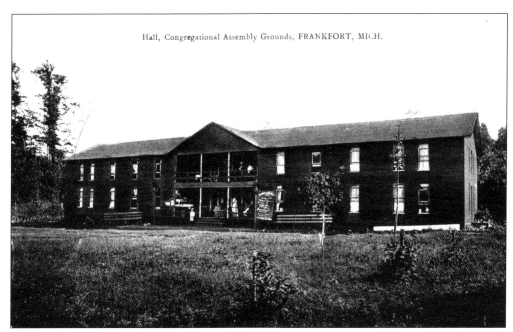

In the earliest years at Frankfort, meetings were held at different hotels, like the Royal Frontenac, and in tents placed at various locations throughout the city. After the lodge, with its 50 bedrooms, was built in 1906 (above), attendance was so great that some by choice and others by necessity continued to stay in tents around the assembly grounds (below). Helping to improve participation were the relatively inexpensive round-trip tickets from Detroit and Toledo, which in 1907 cost between $7 and $9. Round-trip passage on a steamship from Chicago or Milwaukee cost between $5.50 and $7.50, berths costing 75¢ extra and meals 50¢ each. That same year more than 300 persons were registered for the assembly, and numbers grew to over 400 in 1908.

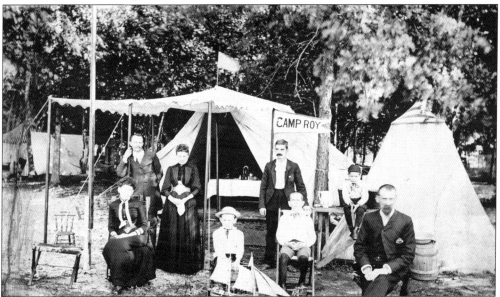

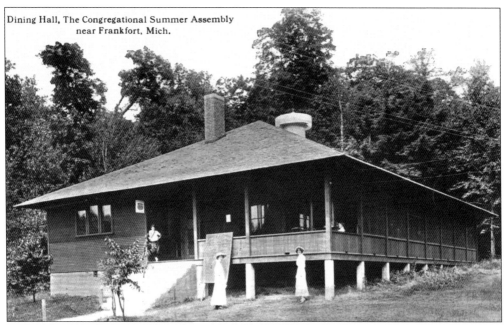

Dining Hall, The Congregational Summer Assembly near Frankfort, Mich.

Both summer and year-round residents were able to participate and enjoy the cultural activities offered by the assembly, which attracted Christians from all Protestant denominations. In addition to the academic lectures on the Bible, morality, and religious topics, there was also a wide variety of music, plays, and dances. Sunday services were always well attended, as were the vesper services on Lake Michigan where a portable organ would be played for the accompaniment. The dining hall, which could accommodate 80 diners, had a screened porch running along the east side overlooking the lake (above). For several years there were annual picnics that alternated between Benzonia and the assembly, celebrating their shared Congregational heritage. However, it must be noted that the rise of the assembly is coincidental to Benzonia being founded as a Congregational colony.

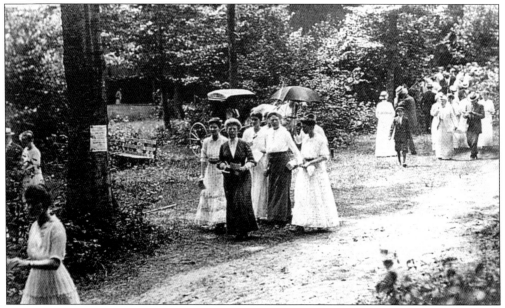

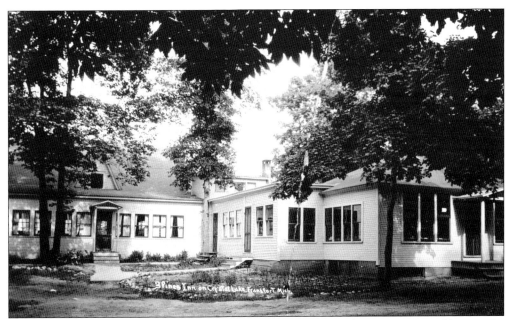

Just to the north and predating Pilgrim and the Congregational Summer Assembly was the development of Crystalia with some of the most advantageous frontage on Crystal Lake. Established by a group of Chicago businessmen who purchased the tract of land from L. W. Crane, a lumberman from South Frankfort, sole ownership eventually passed to one of its members, W. L. Davis, who gave the settlement its name and named the streets. Davis subdivided the tract and sold parcels to wealthy businessmen, including Arthur Brink of Brink's Express. In 1899, he built his own cottage, which he named Three Pines; it became the Three Pines Inn after a dining room was started. It was sold in the 1920s to F. L. Marker of Detroit, who expanded the resort with a grocery and bakery. The Three Pines Inn and its Sunday chicken dinners were a weekly event for those in Crystalia and at the assembly, as well as those boating in from other locations around the lake.

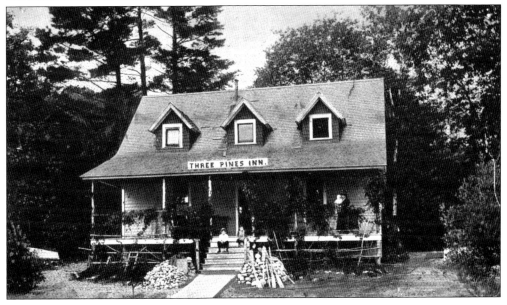

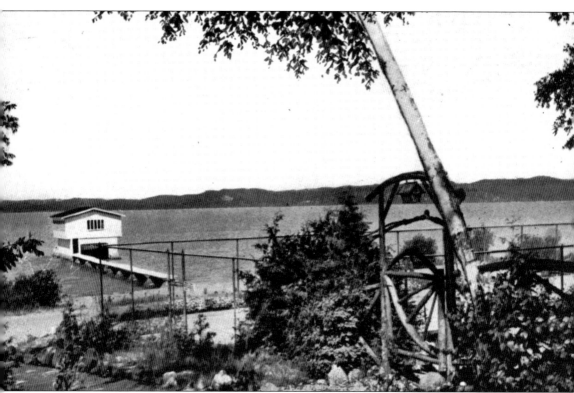

In addition to giving land to the Congregational Summer Assembly at Pilgrim, the Ann Arbor Railroad also gave 160 acres of land to the Disciples of Christ to build its Christian Assembly resort along the south shore. In 1918, the Christian Missionary Society conducted the first session at the Christian Assembly, which was a training camp for church and Bible school officers and leaders. They believed that as World War I raged, "great conferences for prayer and preparation" were needed in a quiet retreat, away from the city, "where there is pure air, sunshine and beautiful scenery in every direction." In its first years, funds were given by the people of Frankfort to help build the accommodations, and the Michigan Christian Missionary Society provided the means, room, and tents for all the participants. Soon after, lodges were built and wells sunk, and by 1922, 400 people were summering for a time at the Christian Assembly, many of whom resided in the nearby resorts around the lake.

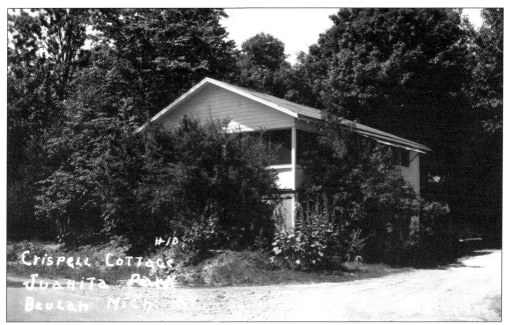

Because the railroad and the larger towns lay on the southern shore of Crystal Lake, and navigable roads around the lake were later in coming, the northern shore was slower to develop and developed differently when growth did come in the second decade of the 20th century. Rather than depend on steamships and passenger cars to bring resorters, the north shore grew with and depended on the family automobile. Place names associated with the north shore, like Oberlin, Glen Malier, Glen Eyrie, the Crispell Cottage at Juanita (above), and Applehof's Blue Heaven (below), are more accurately family compounds and collections of subdivisions than full-blown resorts with hotels, cabins, dining halls, and pavilions.

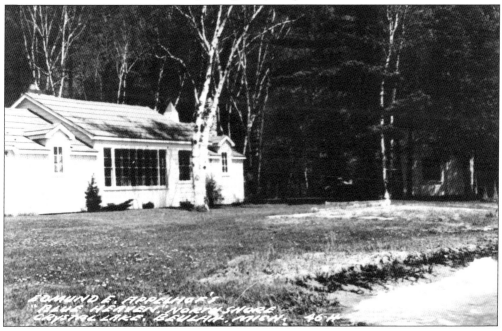

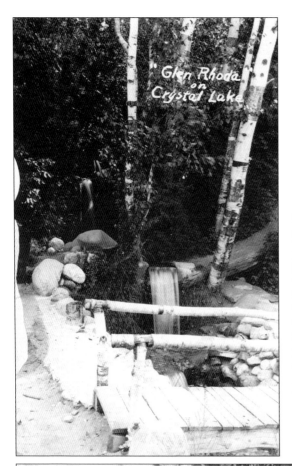

Glen Rhoda was named after the daughter of J. B. Walker, one of Benzonia's original settlers and the first president of the Grand Traverse College. It was more a popular roadside picnic ground and park run by Charles Case of Benzonia. Its chief attraction was a cascading stream that fell in stages from a 70-foot bluff. Picnic tables were provided and were well used, as were campsites and rowboats for fishing. A small refreshment stand, known for its pancakes, also offered soft drinks, ice cream, candy, and picnic supplies. It was also the site of a gas engine boat that could be chartered for trips around the lake, as well as boats for rent.

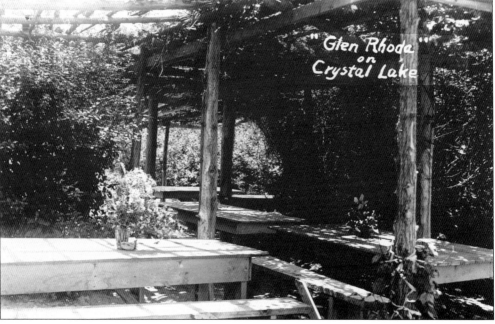

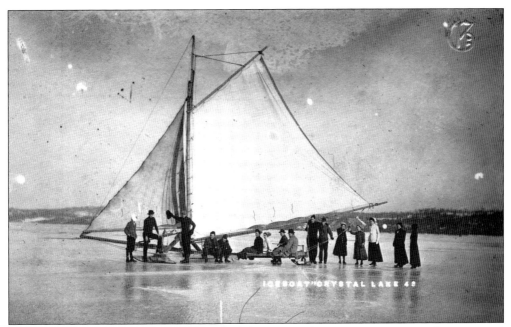

Until Crystal Mountain, at the east end of the county, began to prosper as a ski resort and snowmobiling gained popularity, most vacationers left the lake in the fall. However, year-round residents took advantage of the lake in all seasons. Much more common than iceboating (above) was ice fishing (below). With solid ice, shanties were pulled onto the lake with horses, tractors, or cars. Protected from the wind, many happy hours were spent in the relatively warm hovels with a favorite warming drink. The collection of shanties was referred to as "Smelt Town" and "Shanty Town," with electric lights run out to the little village.

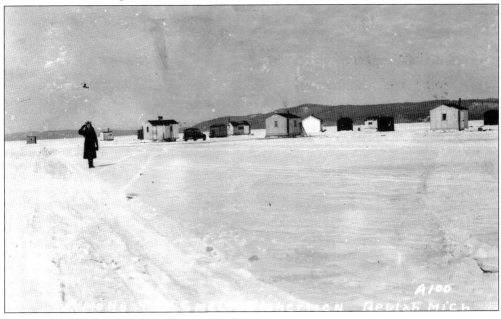

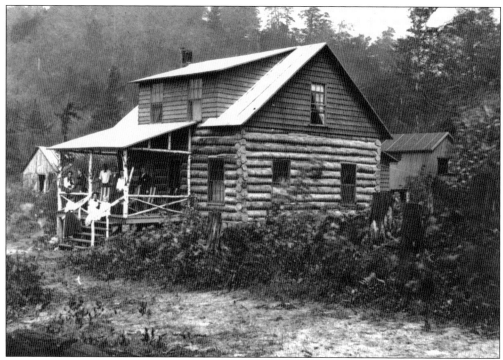

Seeking hardwood lumber for the Piqua Handle Company, in which he was a partner, Olin Rogers of Thompsonville retained some of the property bought by the corporation on the bluff between Crystal Lake and Lake Michigan. The first family home was built there in 1907 (above), but not until the turmoil of the Depression, after unsuccessfully having tried farming around Crystal Lake, did Olin's wife, Leola, begin to rent rooms as a boardinghouse for her acquaintances. She named the lodge Chimney Corners for the four stone fireplaces. More cabins were built during World War II, including Hillside in 1942 (below). After the war and the end of gas rationing, the resort prospered.

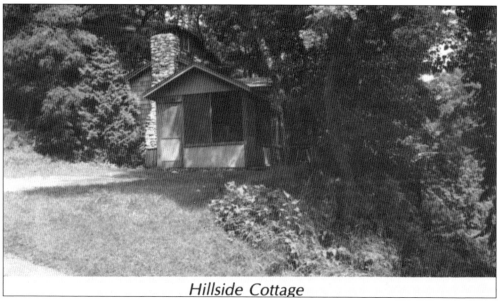

Hillside Cottage

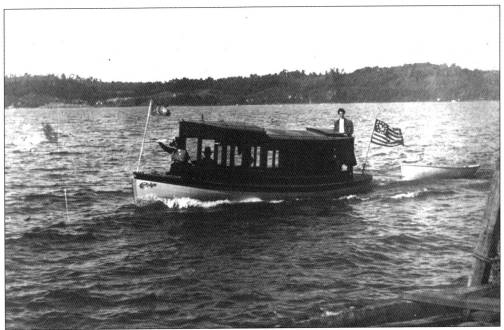

Even before the Chimney Corners Resort opened as such in 1935, Olin Rogers needed transportation for his family between his farm, Orchard Hills, and Beulah, and so he built the *Carolyn*. The launch was docked at Terp's in Beulah and was used to shuttle passengers to Crystalia, near the Rogers home, for a round-trip fee of 25¢.

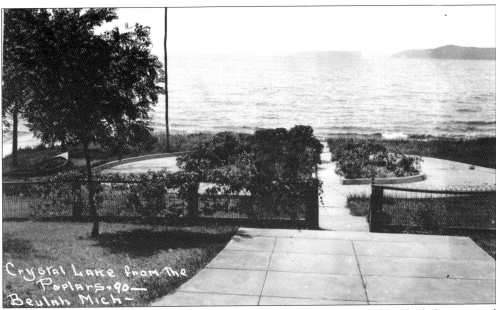

As beautiful as the grounds and lake were, before the 1950s it was unusual for the ladies to spend much time in the out-of-doors. A resort owner reports that patrons chose to take full advantage of the indoor accommodations, and at Chimney Corners, be fed three gargantuan meals a day. After their meals they would sit on the porch, rocking and enjoying the view.

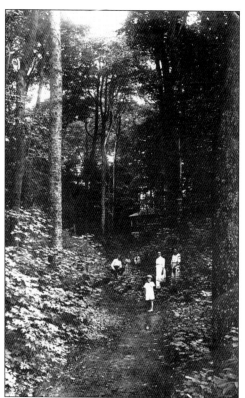

On a postcard depicting this photograph, L. E. Rogers, one of the pioneers of the Congregational Summer Assembly, apologizes for his delay in arriving at the recipients' home. It was, he wrote, "so wonderfully beautiful. I could not leave." A glimpse of the cottage in which he stayed on the assembly grounds is barely visible among the trees and ferns of the bluff.

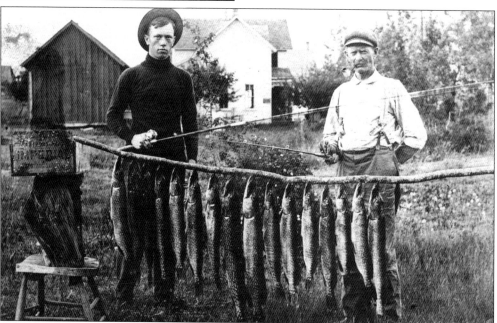

Whether dropping a line for perch off the dock, boating out to the deep waters for pike and sturgeon, wading and casting in the streams that fed the lake for trout, or lounging on the beach with a reel in the sand, Crystal Lake and the smaller lakes surrounding it readily provided the sportsman a chance to take a souvenir snapshot of his catch.

Four
FRANKFORT AND ELBERTA

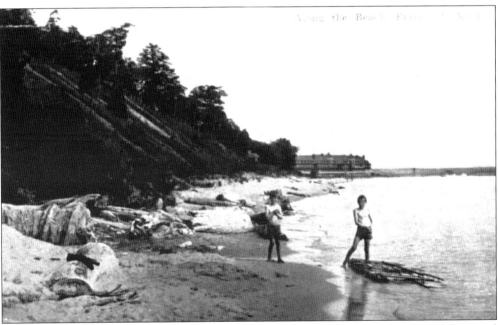

Two boys take their raft out onto Lake Michigan on the Frankfort beach in front of the Royal Frontenac Hotel. Hidden from view by the dune, Frankfort boasts a unique place in Michigan tourism and industry by bordering three bodies of water: Lake Michigan to the west, Crystal Lake to the north, and Betsie Lake to the south. Betsie Lake forms a natural harbor, and with surrounding lands rich in timber, opportunity beckoned those who sailed the Michigan shoreline. After the lumber era, the forests and waters continued to attract entrepreneurs and settlers. Just beyond the Royal Frontenac on the other side of the channel are the ferry docks and iron works of South Frankfort, now known as Elberta.

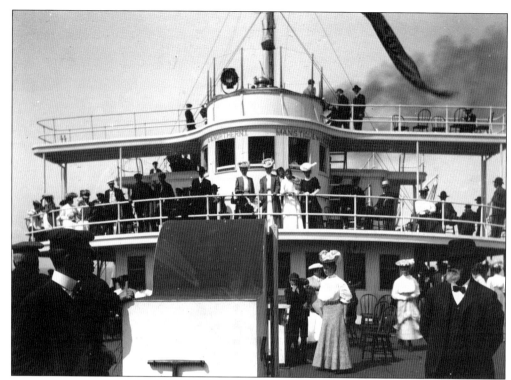

Getting to Crystal Lake was half the fun for travelers, especially those onboard the ships that would dock in Frankfort. The *Manistique, Marquette, and Northern No. 1* sometime before 1909 (above), later named the *Milwaukee*, steams across Lake Michigan with its passengers. Just to the north of the Frontenac, and a few steps from the steamship dock that sat to the east, was the Ann Arbor Railroad's Frankfort depot (below). It was from this depot that passengers could catch the Ping Pong train to the resorts and hotels along the southeast shore of Crystal Lake. The railroad also maintained a line that continued north from the depot along the Lake Michigan beach to allow railroad executives to deliver their private parties directly to their summer homes along the shore.

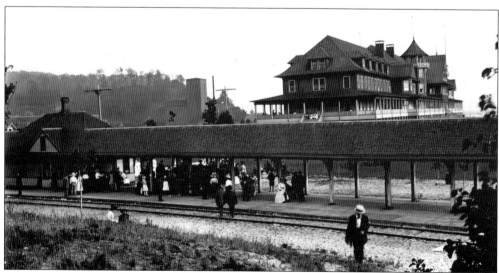

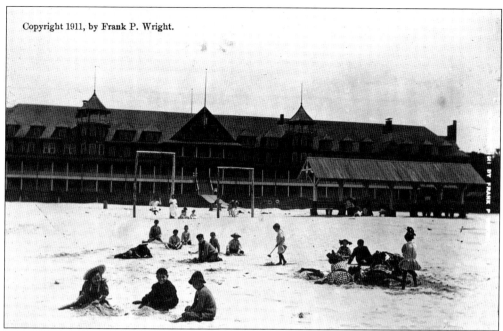

The Royal Frontenac Hotel was opened in 1901 by the Ann Arbor Railroad to increase passenger traffic on its line between Toledo and Frankfort. Over 500 feet long with a wraparound porch on two levels, and containing over 250 rooms, it was one of the largest buildings on Lake Michigan. People came for the cool lake breezes, which are apparently blowing as these children play on the beach in coats.

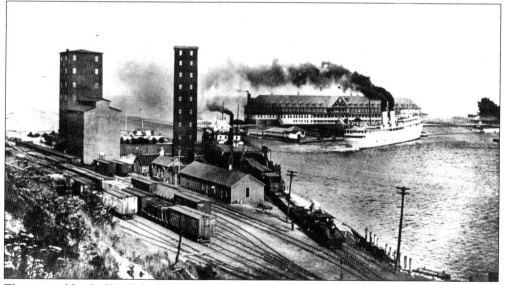

The unique blend of Frankfort's industry and tourism is illustrated by the passenger ship *Northland* docking at the Royal Frontenac Hotel to the north, while the Ann Arbor Railroad ferries take on freight cars across the channel in what was then called South Frankfort. The Frankfort train depot is just able to be seen on the far right. The origin of the settlement's name is uncertain. One explanation states that the view of the bay nestled among rolling hills reminded a German ship captain of Frankfurt-am-Main.

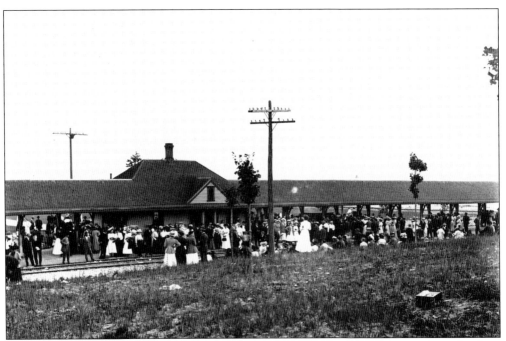

When the season was over, those traveling by train would mass at the depot where the Ann Arbor Railroad would put on as many as 12 passenger cars to begin moving the people home to Detroit, Toledo, and beyond. Also heading back were the 100–150 students of Fisk University in Tennessee who found summer employment at the hotel as porters and waitstaff.

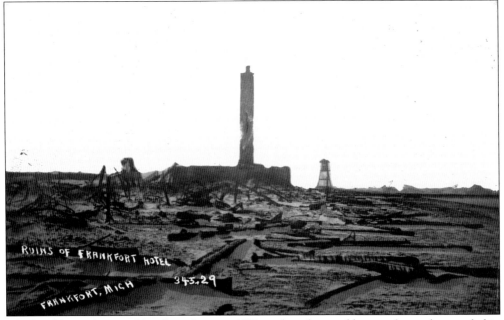

The hotel burned on a cold night in January 1912, with widespread looting famously recorded in a poem that described a mattress being dragged down the beach and prunes, beans, and frozen vinegar carried off. After a police investigation, the Ann Arbor Railroad's property was returned by the looters, who were each fined $9.10 by the justice of the peace.

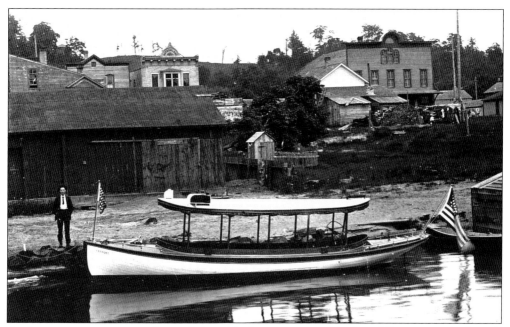

As there were no resorts on Betsie Lake with the exception of the Royal Frontenac, the launch *Vermont* could be hired out of Frankfort to ferry people between Frankfort and South Frankfort, or as far up the Betsie River as was navigable depending on the season and river debris. The Sutherland Saloon (left, semicircle on facade) dates this picture from before 1889.

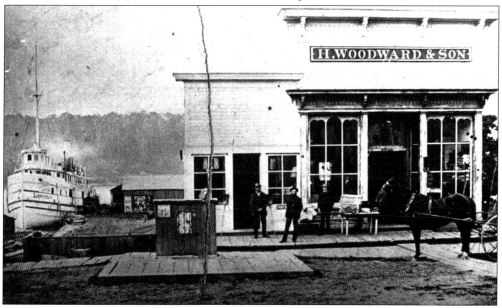

Standing on the south side of Main Street was the Woodward and Son store started by Henry Woodward from Somersetshire, England. A successful land speculator in southern Michigan, he came to Frankfort in 1867, started a dock on Betsie Lake, and ran a small farm where his wheat was the first in the area to be threshed by a machine. After these successes and ever the businessman, he built a mercantile store at his lakeside dock, which he ran until his death in 1889.

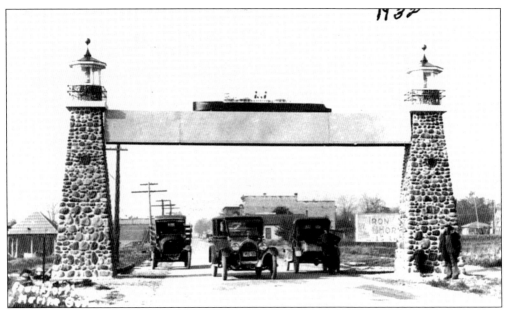

The Frankfort Gateway has been a landmark since 1925, when the first one was constructed on Main and Seventh Streets to honor the Ann Arbor Railroad ferries, which had played such an important role in the town's prosperity. Stones from Lake Michigan were used for the lighthouses that acted as columns, between which sat a model of the *Ann Arbor No. 7*, believed at the time to be the world's most modern and beautiful railroad ferry. In 1937, when street and sewer modernization required its being removed or moved, a new gateway was built on top of the hill leading into Frankfort. In 1967, a model of the *City of Green Bay* replaced the *Ann Arbor No. 7*.

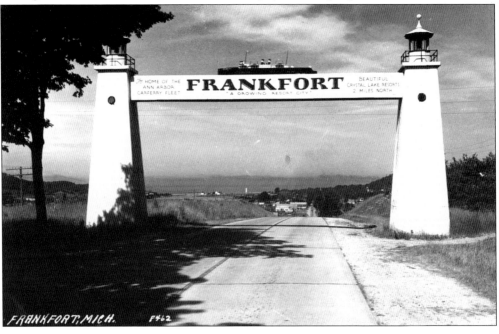

In the later half of the 19th century, Michigan accounted for a little under half of the country's output of salt. Manistee, about 25 miles to the south, was known for a time as Salt City due to its salt wells. In an attempt to cash in on this natural resource (a lumber mill's exhaust steam could be used to extract the salt from the saltwater), mill operator D. B. Butler drilled a 2,000-foot well that resulted in not saltwater but a mineral spring. The sulphur-rich water was famed and used for its healing qualities. For a time, the water was piped to the Royal Frontenac Hotel, which operated a bathhouse. After the hotel burned, a gazebo was built over the spring, and health enthusiasts take the water to this day.

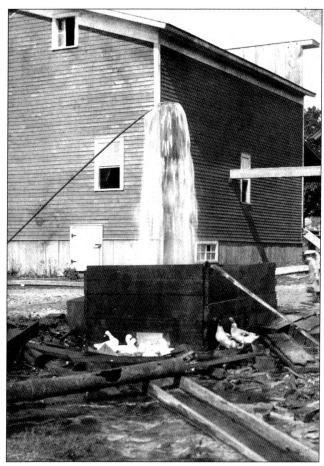

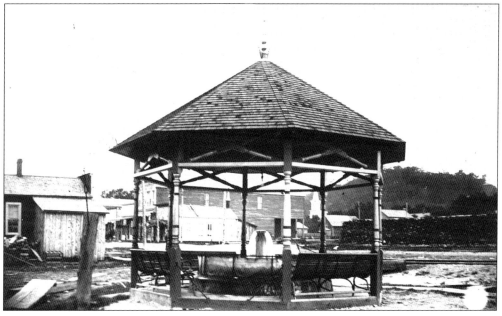

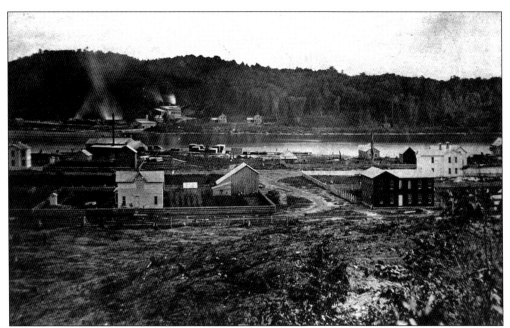

An 1870 picture of Frankfort looks south toward Betsie Lake with the D. B. Butler Mill in the background. The image shows the clear-cutting done around the bay, the houses in town with large gardens and barns, and fencing to keep animals out as much as in. Across the bay is seen the Frankfort Iron Works in South Frankfort.

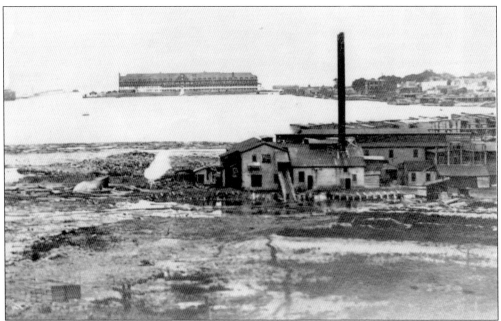

With the amount of timber shipped through Frankfort Harbor, businesses utilizing the raw material sprung up such as Knapp's Woodenware factory (foreground). Knapp's manufactured wooden bowls and butter dishes. The Royal Frontenac Hotel (background) rests on what locals called "the island," which was actually a peninsula between the Betsie Lake and Lake Michigan.

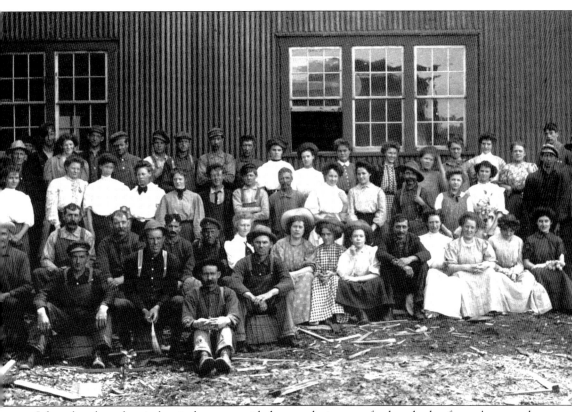

Jobs related to the timber industry provided a steady income for hundreds of people around Crystal Lake for the last half of the 19th century and the first quarter of the 20th. Typical were the mix of men and women, immigrants and native born, who assembled at the mills and factories, such as those at Knapp's Woodenware factory. Identified here are Mike Herban, John Johnson, Art Hollenbeck, Paul Mealey, Ole Didrickson, Mr. Straubel, Rena Johnson, Flocile Burgess, Ruth Meredith, Flossie Oliver, Anna Loefsgard-Flath, Ollie Cooper-Green, Mary Mathewson, Olga Johnson-Shorter, Edith Gunderson-Hansen, Gertie Anderson-Telleson, Lottie Johnson-Sjoholm, Oliver Frederickson, Ben Smith, Clark Benton, Maude Wood-Robinson, Nettie Conner-Prout, Joe Morenzie, Lucy Deeker, Verna De Clair-Zimmerman, Bob Mauseth, Gundson Hollenbeck, Harry Jeffs, Wilda Syers, Henry Adams, Elbert Setterbo, Dolf Adams, Herb Hammond, Viola Voorhuis, Molly De Clair, Mrs. Ike Plont, Hattie Little, Ethel Shafford, Grace Hammond-Watson, Sylvia Snell, Ruth Hunt, Ruth Dunevant, and Jacob Edenborn.

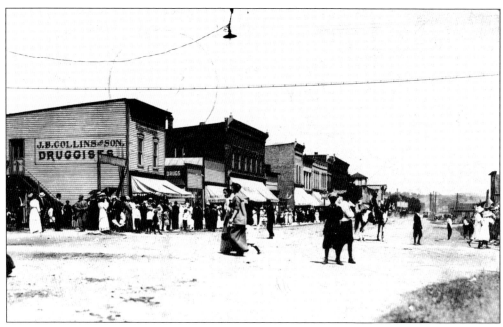

After many years working as a druggist, John B. Collins arrived in Frankfort in 1868 to start the town's first drugstore. His son, Roy Collins, inherited the business in 1901, the storefront becoming a fixture on Main Street (above). An upstairs room was used as city hall and the courtroom, with the justice of the peace sometimes fetching jurors from among the customers at the store's soda fountain. Roy Collins, pictured in both photographs on pages 113 and 114, was very active in the civic life of Frankfort and served as the president of the State Savings Bank. Standing in front of the store (below, from left to right) are Charley Smith the barber, Mangus Anderson, and George "the Greek," who was well known for the candy he made at Collins's.

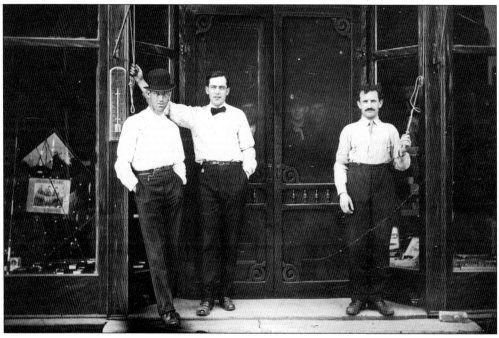

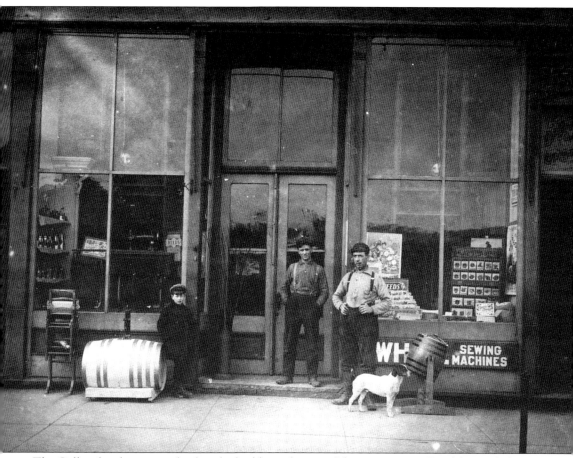

The Collier family was involved in the building of many of the structures in Frankfort including their handsome hardware store, pictured above. Charles Collier Sr. was also instrumental in establishing the lifesaving stations along the Great Lakes' coasts. His sons, Charles, Harry, and Barney, worked as builders, inspectors, and public officials. In a photograph from 1900, Fred Smith (in front of door) is pictured with Harry Collins (right).

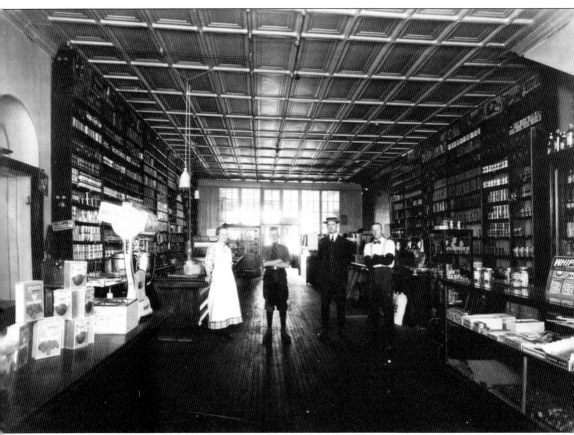

Perhaps the oldest building in Frankfort is the Olsen-Sayles building, which changed hands many times since 1868 when the Prussian-born Fred Kern operated a general store there. In 1909, it was sold to the Frederick-Sayles Company; the new owner Milt Frederick (right) stands with his wife (far left), with perhaps Nelson Sayles (second from right).

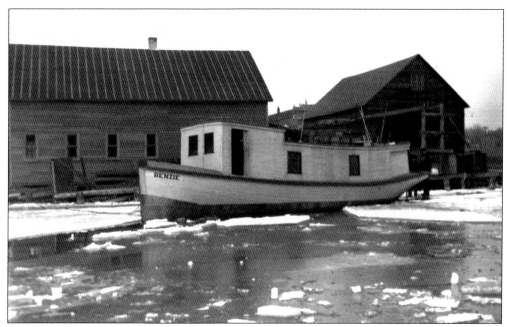

Commercial fishing is as old as Frankfort, as Joseph Oliver, its first European settler, was a fisherman. With the arrival of the Oliver Rubier family in 1870, commercial fishing lasted in Frankfort until it was supplanted by sport fishing in the 1960s. Seeking trout, white fish, and chubbs proved to be a prosperous yet dangerous profession. By 1920, there were 14 separate fishing businesses in operation, with docks along the north shore of Betsie Lake bearing such names as Rodal, Anderson, Olsen, and Bohnow. Whatever the season, with open water the fishing boats and tugs set out to find their catch.

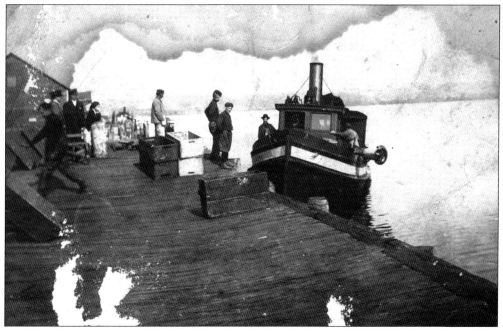

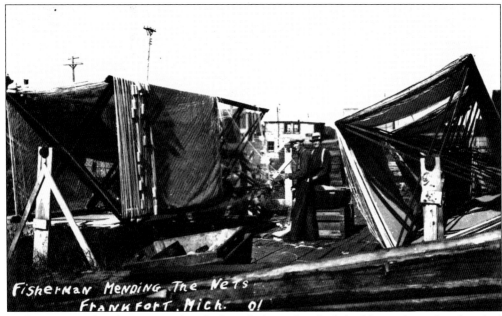

Fisherman Mending The Nets
Frankfort, Mich. 01

Each morning after they returned with their day's catch, which had been cleaned and packed in ice on the boats, boiling water was poured over the nets to kill those organisms that might cause the netting material to rot. The nets were then stretched over reels along the docks to dry in the air and sun, where afternoons were spent repairing whatever damage may have occurred with the morning's activity. Meanwhile the iced fish were taken to the docks and depots where steamships and locomotives would transport the fresh catch to Chicago, Detroit, and as far away as New York.

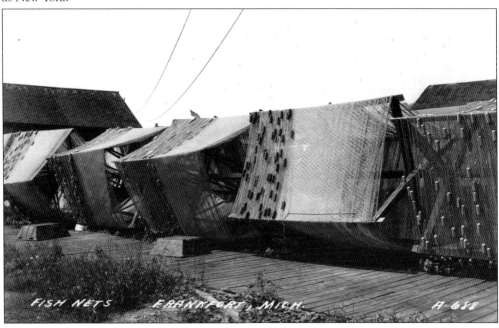

Fish Nets Frankfort, Mich. A-688

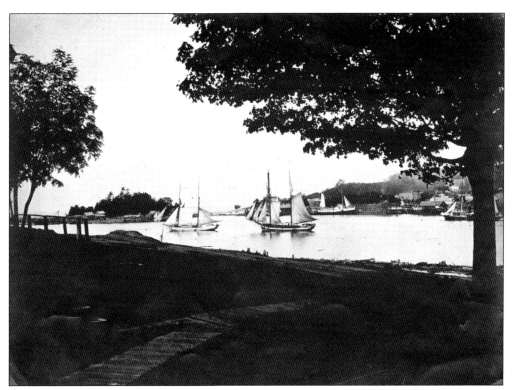

Developed by the Frankfort Land Company beginning in 1859, Frankfort-on-the-Lake, as it was originally called, was a natural choice for the development of industry as Betsie Lake formed a natural harbor. After the Civil War (1861–1865), lumbering began in earnest in northwest Michigan, and Frankfort, resting as it did on Lake Michigan, became a center of activity with several lumber mills, factories, and fishing enterprises. A view of Frankfort Harbor from 1889 (above) shows the sailing ships in the harbor. A photograph from about 1895 (below) shows the Butler Mill with the smokestack, the Forest Avenue Hotel (upside down L to the left of the mill), and the Congregational church (center right).

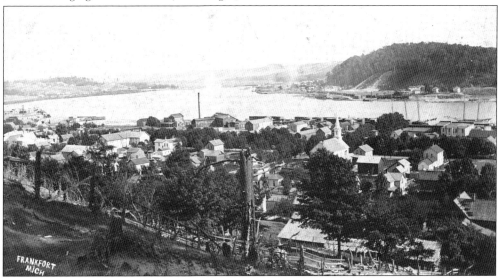

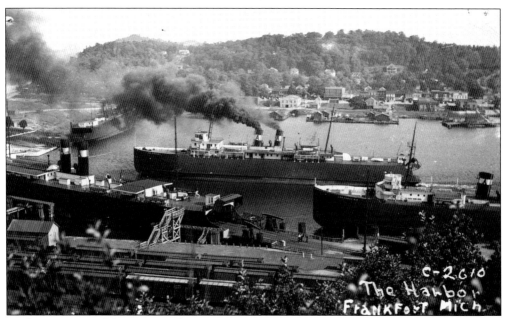

In the 1890s, Frankfort increased in importance as a center of industry when the Ann Arbor Railroad car ferries began to transport railroad cars across Lake Michigan. To avoid the bottleneck of the Chicago yards, the railroad offered a bypass to shippers seeking to deliver their goods westward by creating the world's first railroad ferry transport to cross such a large body of water. Their venture proved very successful for over 90 years with their eventual fleet of ferries running between Frankfort and Manitowoc, Kewaunee, Green Bay in Wisconsin, and Manistique in the Upper Peninsula of Michigan. The downside of the endeavor came in the winter when freezing waters and ice floes could block or endanger the ferries. Many stories are told of the hazards involved in winter shipping, including sinkings and getting trapped in the ice.

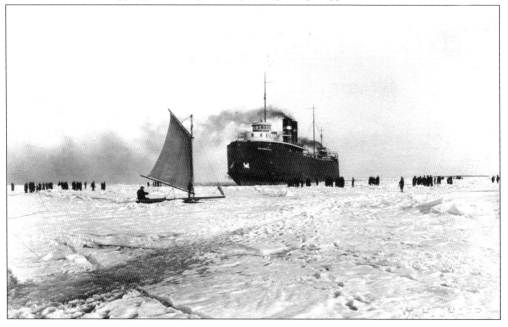

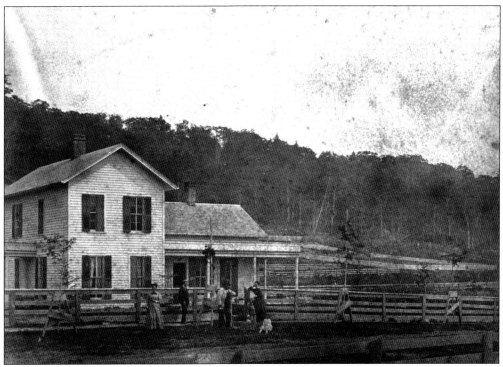

One of the oldest pictures of Frankfort is of the house built by the Frankfort Land Company, taken in 1865. Eugene Frost, whose brother George was a principal stockholder in the company, was sent as the agent to handle the sales and to oversee the development of the harbor. He later turned to real estate and fruit growing.

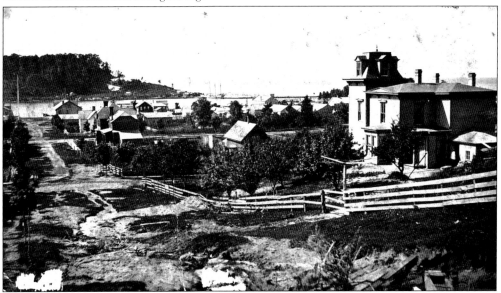

An early view of Frankfort's streets and harbor shows a three-masted ship in South Frankfort. The streets of the sandy soil in the hilly town would frequently wash away and become rutted after heavy rains, making any form of travel other than walking difficult. Town homes all had their small orchards, as did the Upton House (right).

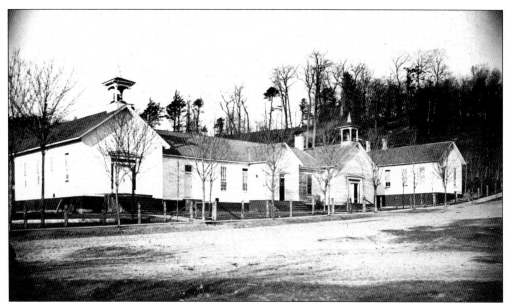

One of the more unusual buildings in Frankfort was the school on Sixth Street, built in 1868 (above). When a larger, new school was built in 1894, the old building served many purposes. The Benzie County Normal School (for educating teachers) occupied the southern section (left), the library was accessed through the central doors, and the northern portion was used for public meetings and, for a time, a jail. A view of the building from on top of the ridge (below) shows the Butler Mill in the background. Notice the outhouse in the center of the picture, against the fence.

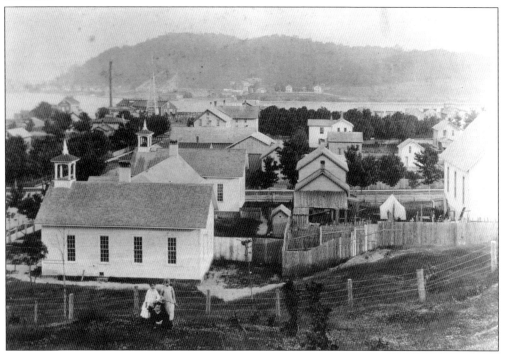

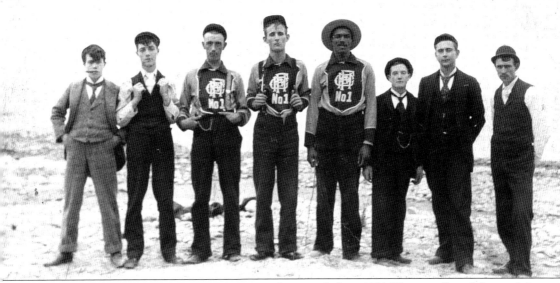

Frankfort's fire department is seen posing in a photograph from 1891. They are (from left to right) Dud Collins, Joe Weghoff, Harry Collier, Henry Michael, Art Skinner, Roy Collins, Claude Whelbesk, and Lou Sutherland. As in most towns built from lumber, fire was a constant danger, and many homes and businesses were lost to open-flame lighting and heating.

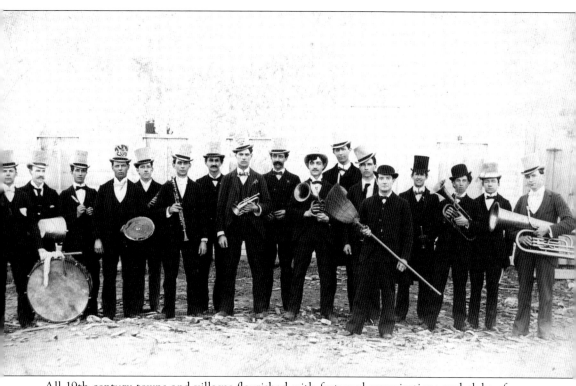

All 19th-century towns and villages flourished with fraternal organizations and clubs of every sort. In 1891, the Alpha Club, which at least had elements of a band, included Tom Storr, Archie Upton, Michael Carland, Charley Jenks, Roy Collins (with broom), Harry Smith, George Moore, Joe Wyckoff, Al Wyckoff, Will Bratt, Max Racheil, Frank Snider, Ted Upton, Lorenzo Potter, Julian Frost, Charley Carland, and George Sites.

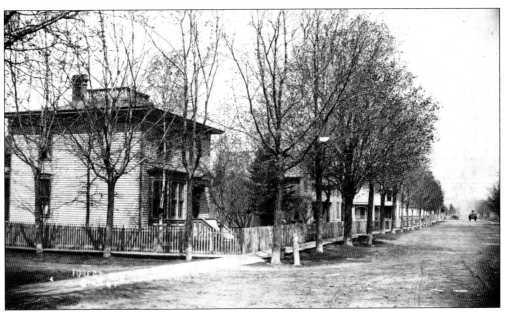

With its steelworks, mills, factories, fishing, lumber, and railroad, Frankfort was established as a prosperous town. The money from these industries allowed residents to build stately Victorian homes along tree-lined boulevards, such as those on Forest Avenue (above) and, with its houses perched high on a ridge with spacious and slopping front lawns, Leelanau Avenue (below). The publicity generated by the Ann Arbor Railroad for the Royal Frontenac Hotel caused the population to explode, filling the entire town for the summer season. To meet the demand and make some extra money, many families rented out their large homes and lived in small houses built on the back of their property.

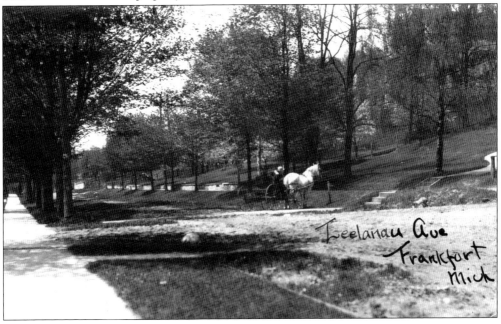

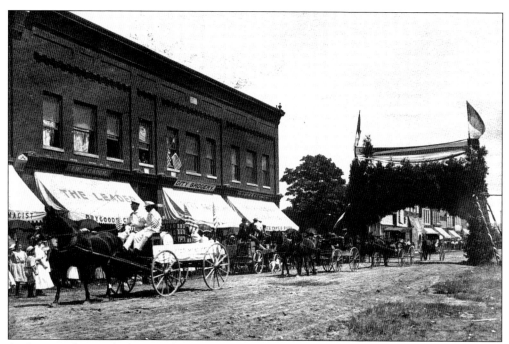

A photograph records the Fourth of July parade down Frankfort's Main Street in 1906. An arch in the center of the road seems to foretell the gateway that would be built on the east end of the street 19 years later. Among the stores pictured are Glarem and Classens (right) and City Grocery (center), two long-lived Frankfort businesses in a building rebuilt in 1903 after a fire.

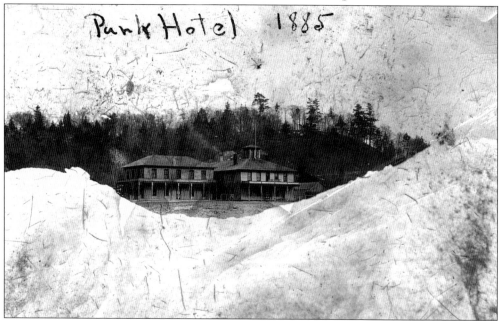

Originally built as the Delbridge House in 1867, the Park Hotel was purchased by the Chambers family in 1877. Sitting across from the Frankfort City Park, here in a winter scene, its guests were required to participate in the American plan, which meant that all their meals were taken at the hotel.

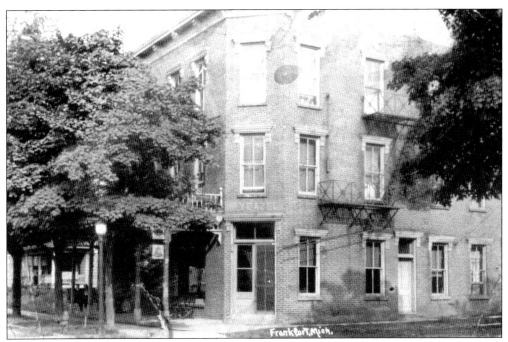

Built in 1867, the Frankfort House was the hotel patronized by lumberjacks as they began to move out in the spring, and from whom it was reportedly difficult to collect the money due. Along with the Royal Frontenac, the Yeazel, as it was then called, was among the leading area hotels. It burned in 1927.

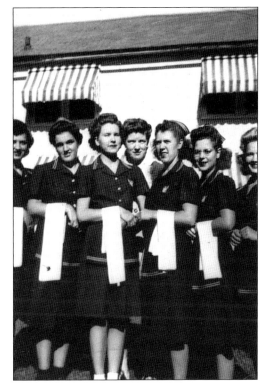

The waitstaff from the Koch Hotel, including Agnes Baker (second from left) and Natalie Koch (fourth from left), stands ready to serve up the hotel's famous Hungarian goulash and Yankee pot roast. A smaller, more exclusive hotel with only 10 rooms, its dining room was crowded during the summer evening where over 200 dinners were served.

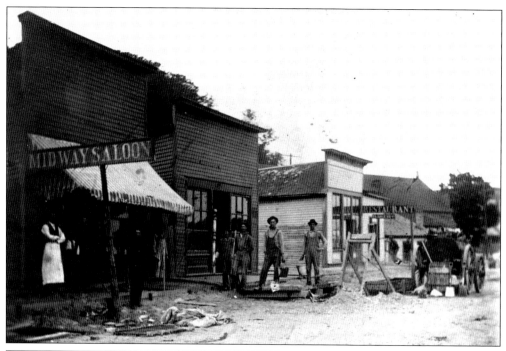

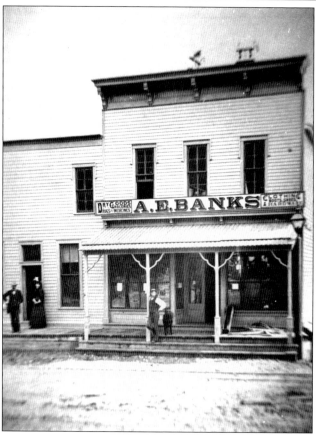

Across the channel from Frankfort lay South Frankfort, which was the site of the Ann Arbor Railroad ferry docks, as well as the site for mills, factories, and food-processing plants. It quickly prospered and was laying its first sidewalk in 1894 (above). The Midway Saloon's bartender John Rossidor (left, with apron) looks on as Ed and Raleigh Ward (center, with buckets) and John Schaeffer (white overalls) labor. The Smith Barber Shop and Mrs. Dundon's Bakery and Restaurant (with city sprinkler parked in front) also benefited from the improvement. Among Elberta's businesses was the A. E. Banks general store. It was originally started by Thomas Anderson, who had moved to Elberta from Detroit with the Peninsular Iron Works in 1868. When the ironworks collapsed, Anderson started his grocery store, selling it to Banks in 1878.

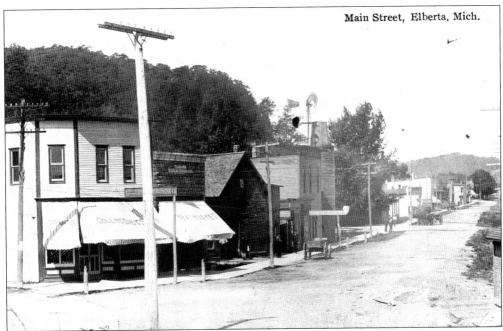

Main Street, Elberta, Mich.

Named for a variety of peach that dominated area orchards for a time, Elberta's canning and packing plants rested on the southeast shore of Betsie Lake. In a scene that predates 1911 (above), the main street of Elberta is seen with its businesses. In 1904, Roy Collins of J. B. Collins and Son, druggists, followed a common practice among Frankfort businessmen like Glarem and Classens and opened a satellite store (left) across the bay in South Frankfort, where it remained in operation for 16 years. Down the street (out of sight behind the tree above, and below) was the American House. Built in 1877, it served chiefly as a hotel for lumbermen until the end of the lumber era, when it ceased operating as a hotel. Through the 1940s, it housed the township library, election hall, and public meeting hall until it was torn down in 1972.

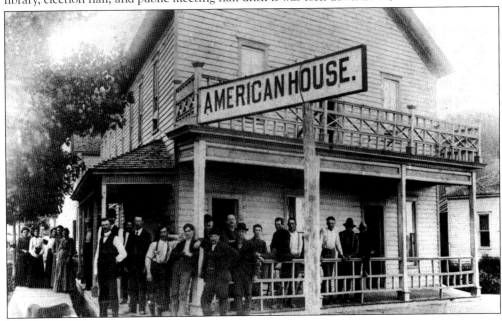

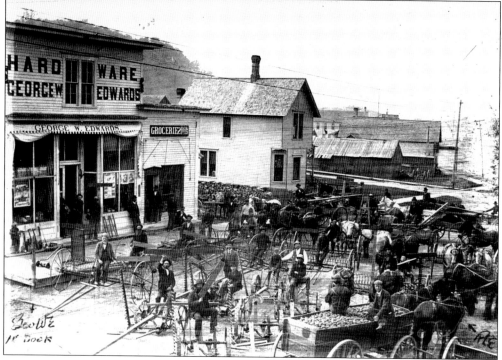

In 1898, George W. Edwards bought the company store and office building of lumberman L. W. Crane and turned it into a hardware store. Edward's Hardware was known miles around for its farm implements, as is seen in this photograph from 1903–1904 with the large delivery of "Plano Machines," used for harvesting grasses and grains. The second floor of the building also served as a roller rink and for the manufacture of wagon boxes.

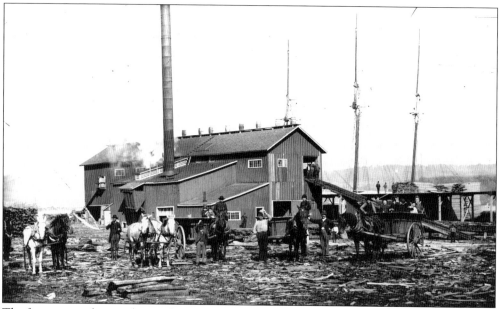

The first man to clean and open the Betsie River to logging was Lawrence W. Crane, an Irishman who first came to the area in the late 1860s. By the 1880s, after reverses and successes, he rose to be the leading lumberman of South Frankfort. The operation continued until shortly after his death in 1905, when the timber played out.

The Norwegian immigrant Ragnar Robertson, who came to Elberta from Minnesota in the 1920s, created the Elberta Mountain Winter Sports Park to stimulate interest and enthusiasm for ski jumping. By late February 1950, the site was ready for jumping. However, since no residents knew how to do it, and Robertson had not done it since his youth in Norway, the winter passed without its being put to use. The following winter, after gaining some experience at a smaller jump north of Empire, the area's youth began using the jump. For several years, Elberta hosted a winter carnival with ski jumping exhibitions that attracted skilled participants from around the country. After a brief period of expansion, with more runs developed and tow ropes installed, interest in the activity waned, and by 1962, the park was phased out.

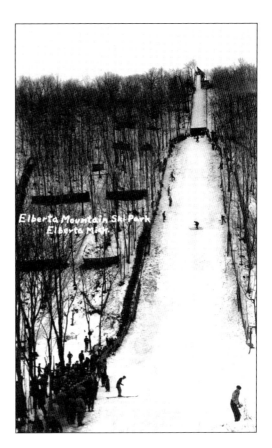

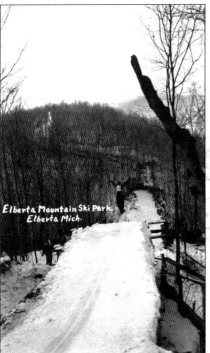

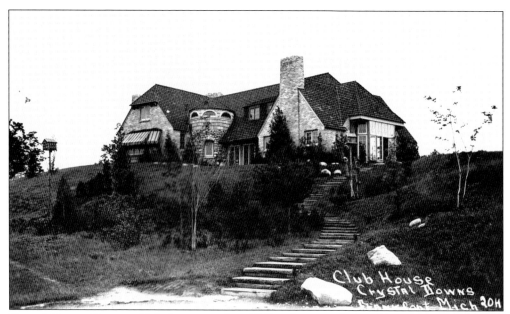

Crystal Downs Country Club first opened in 1928 with a nine-hole golf course and greens fee of $1.50. Soon after, famed golf course architects Dr. Alister MacKenzie and Perry Maxwell were hired to design the course. At first reluctant to design a course in northern Michigan, MacKenzie's visiting the sight with its view of Lake Michigan and Crystal Lake changed his mind. His philosophy of design, in an era before large-scale earth-moving equipment was used for golf courses, was to imitate and blend in with the natural beauty and lay of the land. Finished in 1933, it has consistently been ranked among the top 10 golf courses in the country.

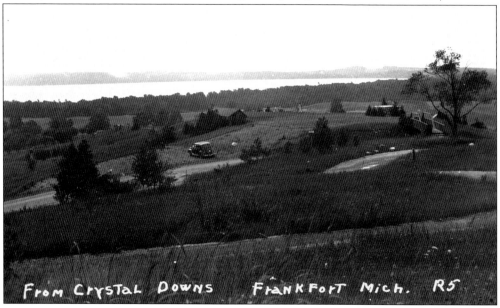

Point Betsie is the most westward point extending into Lake Michigan along the Michigan shore, and the southern point of the Manitou Passage. To guide the ever-increasing lake traffic carrying passengers, merchandise, and raw materials, an 1852 act of Congress ordered a lighthouse be built. Since October 20, 1858, a light has shined from the tower to help give safe passage for the ships and boats on Lake Michigan.

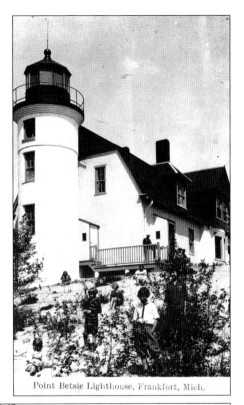
Point Betsie Lighthouse, Frankfort, Mich.

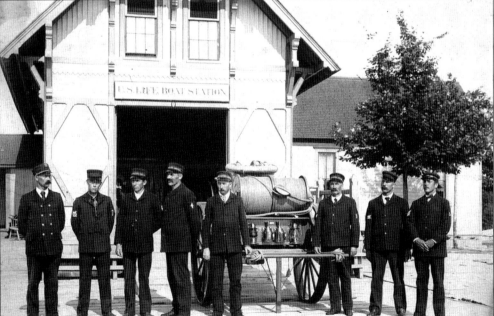
In 1874, Point Betsie was selected as a lifesaving station, the United States Life Saving Service being a precursor to the U.S. Coast Guard. One of the duties of the service was to patrol the beach for several miles in each direction to seek out those ships in distress. A photograph from the 1890s shows the crew members from Point Betsie standing at their station.

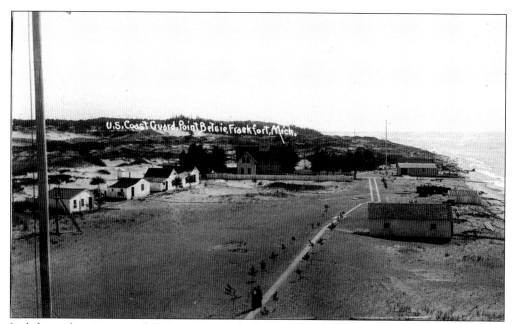

Lighthouse keeping was a full-time job, and the keeper's family lived in the lighthouse. Likewise, those serving in the U.S. Life Saving Service also came to Point Betsie with their families. A postcard from sometime after 1914 shows the Coast Guard station at Point Betsie stretching along the shoreline, complete with the boathouses with tracks to the lake (right), station house (center), and family quarters (left).

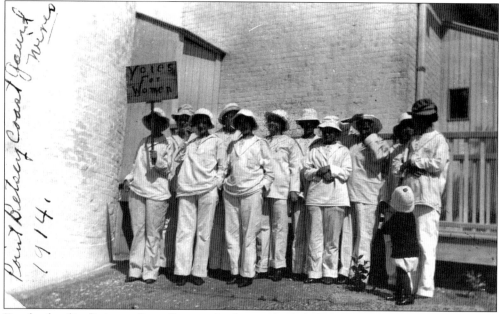

For the families living at Point Betsie, whether at the lighthouse or at the station, it was not uncommon for the wives and children to help out in carrying out the duties. A photograph from 1914, the year the U.S. Life Saving Service became the U.S. Coast Guard, shows the Point Betsie Coast Guard wives dressed in their husbands' uniforms agitating for the right to vote.

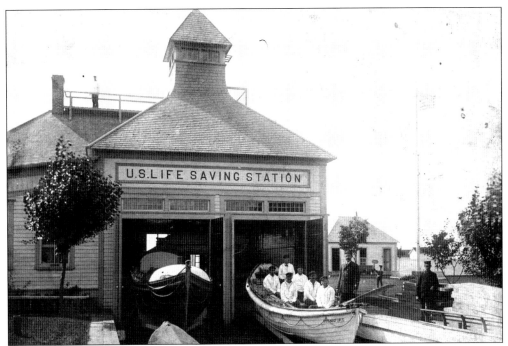

In October 1880, a celebrated rescue occurred one mile south of Frankfort. When the *J. H. Hartzell* went down with its 495 tons of iron ore, all but one of the crew was saved by the members of the Point Betsie station together with the citizens of Frankfort. To further insure the safety of transport, the U.S. Congress authorized a lifesaving station be established in Frankfort in 1882. A photograph form the 1890s (above) shows the crew in its lifesaving boat sitting on the roller tracks. With the Royal Frontenac in the background, members from the Frankfort station do their boat drill (below). Practicing in front of an audience was calculated to increase the prestige of the lifesaving service and perhaps also impress the young women staying at the hotel.

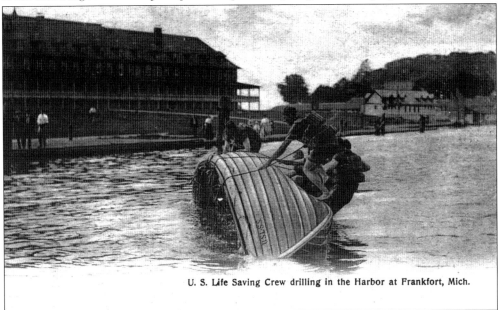

U. S. Life Saving Crew drilling in the Harbor at Frankfort, Mich.

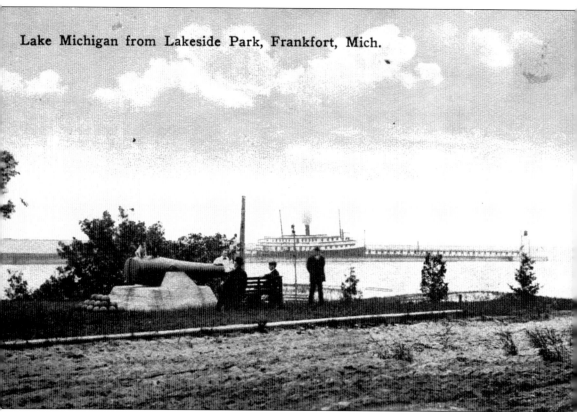

Lake Michigan from Lakeside Park, Frankfort, Mich.

A flyer from the Park Hotel, which sat across from the city park (above), extols the virtues of the fresh air of Frankfort and its beach along Lake Michigan: "Frankfort is ideal for those wishing to escape hay fever. Cool dust-free air from the lake works magic even with stubborn cases. You will be quickly relieved no matter how badly affected when you arrive. The pine-scented air—a bracing tonic that refreshes you for another day—builds up a store of energy and smoothes out frayed nerves." Furthermore, the flyer promises that there is no finer freshwater bathing, that fishing is abundant, and that there are absolutely no mosquitoes, all of which were most assuredly enjoyed by this family on the Lake Michigan beach.

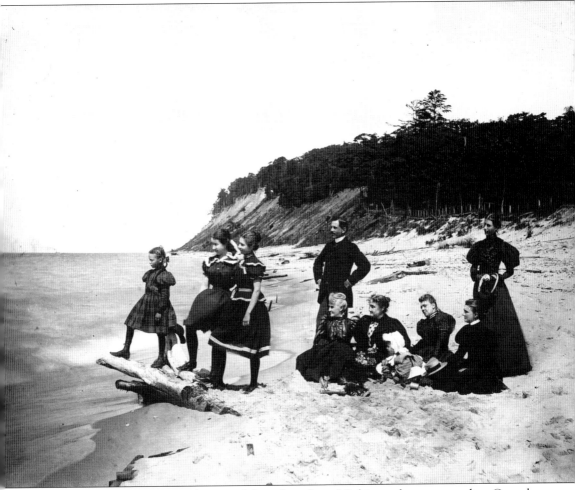

Of the vacation paradises on the many lakes of northern Michigan, those surrounding Crystal Lake are unique in their proximity to the beaches and recreation of the "Big Lake," Lake Michigan. Above, a family poses on the Frankfort beach, while a few hundred yards over the dune and moraine rests Crystal Lake. The evening gathering on the beach to watch the sunset, either at a Sunday vespers organized by the Congregational assembly, or with ones family on the last evening before leaving home, the clinging sand, the feel of the breeze, and the smell of the pine are the enduring memories of generations.

Discover Thousands of Local History Books Featuring Millions of Vintage Images

Arcadia Publishing, the leading local history publisher in the United States, is committed to making history accessible and meaningful through publishing books that celebrate and preserve the heritage of America's people and places.

Find more books like this at
www.arcadiapublishing.com

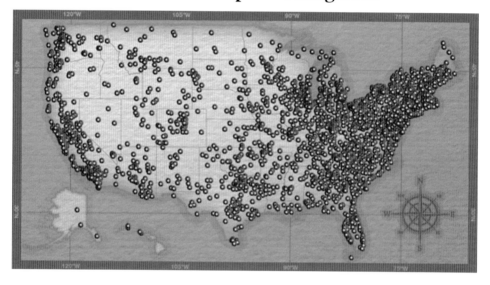

Search for your hometown history, your old stomping grounds, and even your favorite sports team.

Consistent with our mission to preserve history on a local level, this book was printed in South Carolina on American-made paper and manufactured entirely in the United States. Products carrying the accredited Forest Stewardship Council (FSC) label are printed on 100 percent FSC-certified paper.

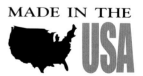